Mix ... ing
in the secondary School

Editors

BRIAN DAVIES and RONALD G. CAVE

Ward Lock Educational

ISBN 0 7062 3648 3

First published 1977

Set in 11 on 13 point Garamond and printed by
Latimer Trend & Company Ltd, Plymouth

for Ward Lock Educational
116 Baker Street, London, W1M 2BB
A member of the Pentos Group
Made in England

Contents

Introduction   v
Brian Davies and Ronald G. Cave

1 Research findings on teaching groups in secondary schools   1
   Peter Corbishley

2 Meanings and motives in 'going mixed ability'   18
   Brian Davies

3 Planning for mixed ability   41
   Bob Gough and Jimmy McGhee

4 Mixed-ability teaching at Hounslow Manor School   55
   John White

5 Mixed ability at Bishop Douglass School   69
   Michael Caulfield

6 Assessment in the mixed-ability group   80
   R. N. Deale

7 Special pupils in mixed-ability groups   98
   D. C. Jones-Davies

Select bibliography   113

Index   115

Introduction

Brian Davies and Ronald G. Cave

Nothing defies a generalization quite like the British educational system. While in Dyfed, mixed-ability grouping may still be pretty much the other man's mania, in London and elsewhere it has become a normal feature of first-year work in secondaries. In some fully reorganized authorities there will be virtually no streaming, banding or setting at this point. Even in authorities some way off complete reorganization (and they still predominate) 40–50 per cent of secondaries commonly have first-year mixed ability. If mathematics and modern languages are excluded, it is just as usual to find 30 per cent continuing with it into the second year and 20 per cent into the third. It is no longer the idiosyncratic choice of individualist head or teacher. To 'go mixed ability' is to make as ordinary and defensible an educational choice as to stream, band or set at this level.

This book aims to begin where the proselytizing ends. Most non-trivial educational innovations pass through an early phase when their legitimacy is highly contested. At this stage, most description and analysis of them is either of a strongly 'pro' or 'con' kind. Honest evaluation of what they have to offer is difficult. Though the contributors to this volume may vary in the precise degree of their enthusiasm for mixed-ability grouping, certain continuities are evident in their work. The first is that mixed ability is no magic wand – indeed there is a real desire to understand and analyse what a change to it *is*, both in school and societal terms. Secondly, proper stress is laid upon the links between motives and objectives which lie behind the choice of mixed ability and the mechanics of practical activity of achieving it and the nature of its outcomes. Thirdly, there is repeated emphasis upon the vital importance of locating tasks and problems at the level of individual schools and teachers, within a local context.

The plan of the book stems from the recent, direct knowledge by contributors of mixed-ability change, gained at school, organizational, administrative, in-service and research levels. Peter Corbishley sets the scene with a piece that sharply focuses upon how historically school grouping practices have responded in changing ways to wider social pressures. He aims to demystify for teachers the 'messages' that lie within changing and apparently contradictory research emphases upon grouping. He shows that there is something to be gained from the changing face of 'the literature' here and in America since the 1920s, if only the realization that the real effect of changing grouping practices stems not simply from changing the labels put upon groups of children, but in altering access to educational experience within individual schools for particular intakes of children. He is deeply sceptical of the usefulness of survey-type approaches in proving anything of real use to teachers at school level. To illustrate the wider social pressures which he sees at work upon changing grouping fashions, he takes Colin Lacey's well-known study of a Northern school. Hopefully, what he has to say will add fresh perspectives to teachers' abilities to grasp the powerful but unseen forces which partly shape and certainly set limits to their own efforts.

Davies's contribution stems largely from work in progress jointly with Peter Corbishley and financed by the Social Science Research Council. This took the form in 1975–76 of a review of secondary school grouping and curricular practices in Greater London. It will go on this year and next in the form of a number of school case studies of teacher strategies and pupil identities in mixed-ability contexts. A number of findings spring very clearly from the first stage of the work: that mixed-ability innovation is very strongly linked with secondary reorganization, that it is to a large degree a 'first-year' change and that it has more to do – as intention and practice – with delay and diagnosis in selection, than with replacing it. It almost always proceeds from a sharply revealed consciousness of the 'bad effects of streaming'. But in the present stage of its development in many schools, it also lacks a clear vision of 'unstreamed' practice. Streaming between classes is too easily replaceable by streaming within, though this in itself may offer gains. They have been impressed by the frequently reiterated benefits claimed to result from a change in 'grouping' alone (that is to say, even where there is still a plain expression of uncertainty about changed classroom 'practice'). These gains centre around pupil morale, motivation and performance. It is also evident that some schools have made solid progress toward rearranging content and teaching approaches in the direction of successful extension of common curriculum. If schools do fail children – and we have tended to see that failure traditionally in terms of unequal access to length of stay, exam opportunities, etc. – then surely it is time to see that failure squarely in terms of differential access to what there is to know.

Bob Gough and Jimmy McGhee wrote their article when co-directors of the Schools' Council Materials for Curriculum Planning Unit. In that capacity, they spent a great deal of their time investigating school change processes, and especially curricular and grouping innovation. They also combine long experience of teaching, teacher-training and in-service work. Their ideas upon planning presuppose a school facing a *de facto* decision to 'go mixed-ability'. They cover the whole spectrum of decisions and problems to be encountered in such a context from 'which abilities are being mixed?' to long-term monitoring of the process. Their main emphasis, characteristically, is upon approaches to the successful achievement of appropriate teaching materials. They highlight the vital role of in-service preparation, particularly the management of in-school training and development. But all this, they insist, rests crucially upon a school having 'a very clear understanding of its reasons for wishing to have mixed-ability groups'.

The two chapters which follow, by the headmasters of Hounslow Manor and Bishop Douglass Schools, illustrate strikingly the complexity of making a mixed-ability choice. John White at Hounslow shows how his school very recently moved from banding. It was hoped that the move would improve motivation and general performance. At the same time, it was made quite quickly and allowed to merge with the wider exigencies of school organization and departmental variation.

Hounslow Manor is, like many schools in Greater London, a bustling, multicultural comprehensive, still waiting for its truly 'balanced' intake. At the moment, it has settled for a lower school mixture of mixed ability with half-year setting, varying by department. Its fourth- and fifth-year arrangements are ones of complex choice and grouping variety. John White is perfectly explicit as to how his 'mixed economy' was reached and his belief in it.

Michael Caulfield at Bishop Douglass School in Barnet describes a situation where the change to mixed ability is of greater antiquity, achieved over a greater time span. Whereas John White's School is a year older as a comprehensive, with its origins in the amalgamation of two fully maintained secondary moderns, Michael Caulfield is head of a voluntary controlled Catholic school formed out of a mixed secondary modern which merged with an independent girls' grammar in 1969. The secondary modern had a history of 'year-themes' curriculum from its inception in 1963 and first attempted mixed ability in 1964. In the beginning this was confined to RE, Creative Arts and PE, of which Caulfield indicatively says that 'we felt that the presence of a few subjects in which wholly mixed-ability teaching occurred would strengthen the "lifting" influence' of mixed-ability forms which already existed for social and pastoral purposes. Amid the 'expected' gains in terms of pupil and staff enjoyment, he equally revealingly says that staff teaching mixed-ability groups, from the start 'talked mainly of individual children while their colleagues with setted groups talked mostly of classes . . . Teachers began to talk to one another about such sacrosanct privacies as how they planned their lessons, what resources they had made or discovered for themselves . . .' In-service work was *ad hoc* – visits elsewhere, internal discussion and helping – but he makes it sound exciting, even passionate. Over a two-year period, mixed ability was taken up by all subjects except mathematics, English and French. There was no 'top-down' imposition but there was, Caulfield claims, a growing belief that mixed ability contributed effectively to child needs. The final switch was made by mathematics as late as 1972. Caulfield implies a natural rightness about the gradualism at Bishop Douglass. The upshots have certainly been low teacher turnover, high quality curriculum and resource preparation and a sixth form of 200 in a six-form entry school. Bishop Douglass has few problems of massive remedial bottom, but it also lacks any extended 'top'. It certainly enjoys real and beneficent parental support, also clearly referred to by John White, alongside what the head describes as the 'determined involvement' of staff.

Both schools have spent a great deal of time rethinking assessment procedures. It might in truth be said, that for far too long, usual secondary school practices in respect of both parents and assessment have had a number of things in common – both have tended to be limited, conventional and lacking in depth. For this reason, we have given a full chapter to Rory Deale on assessment.

Deale argues that the problems of assessing the effectiveness of mixed-ability teaching are, in fact, not different in kind from those which arise from other sorts of grouping, but are rather of degree and urgency. Perhaps the greatest virtue of his piece is to show that an exacting area, all too easily shunned by teachers, is both intellectually accessible and feasible. He refers to the potential loss of structure and traditional support encountered in mixed-ability teaching, especially in a move to individual work. There is an increase in the needs to identify extremes, ensure adequate feedback and evaluate effectiveness (also very much on the mind of John White). Like Gough and McGhee, he emphasizes the importance of knowing what purposes are before, in this case, being in a position to assess 'fitness' of test materials to them. Many may find him healthily reassuring on the wastefulness of overelaboration in the process of creating mixed-ability groups. He says 'there is not much point in trying to achieve a delicately precise balance', given a variety of imponderables, not least the way in which any teaching group takes on its own character after formation. His clear exposition of test criteria and types is as valuable as the pinpointing for teachers of the heart of the problem which is raised by intra-class group variation – that of 'pacing' material across the ability range. We would very much echo his emphasis here. Real pressure upon content is generated for any teacher who in real degree aims at 'common' coverage by a class of widely differing abilities. He concludes with the reminder that an effective assessment programme can only be devised by individual teachers in conjunction with their actual teaching syllabus.

The last chapter, but by no means the least important in terms of the practical problems of mixed-ability schools, is that by Clive Jones-Davies on 'special pupils'. It is clear from his argument as to why he uses this term in preference to the more usual one, 'remedials'. Starting his account with a contrast between the difficulties of primary and secondary schools in respect of 'age/attainment gaps' – by the secondary stage, there are even larger differences in terms of children's interests, attitudes, motivation and literacy than earlier – he carefully distinguishes between six categories of the 'special'. There are ESN(M) and borderline children; those of 'below average ability'; those with specific retardation (either with perceptual difficulties in relation to reading and writing or suffering 'subject alienation'); those with discontinuous educational experience; the maladjusted and the disruptive. For this range, he argues, therapy is not enough. 'Children with learning difficulties may not be "taught at" as may be pupils whose learning abilities are unimpaired. The underlying causes of failure must first of all receive attention so that pupils will be more ready for teaching.' Personal programmes are required, on an individual not block-withdrawal basis, against a background of attempted integration of their work and presence in the general mixed-ability groups. Three levels of remedial action are required: in respect of specific skill weaknesses, literary and numeracy, and 'catching up'. He wants to see this organized in an Extra Learning Centre in each school – a more than usually felicitious euphemism for a remedial department which operates firmly in conjunction with both academic departments, advising on preparation of special materials for use in ordinary classroom contexts, as well as withdrawing individuals where more appropriate. The Centre would rely upon external specialists like educational psychologists and draw upon the help of parents and older pupils.

Note that Clive Jones-Davies points out very clearly in the first section of his piece that 'one teacher's mixed-ability group is another's slow learning group or A stream'. What he is clearly alluding to, is that the size of the remedial or extra-learning problem facing different schools varies widely, in both relative and absolute terms, depending upon the range and shape of their individual ability and social intakes. Many schools, overwhelmed by the sheer size and weight of their less-able intakes, may view his proposals as a counsel of perfection. They believe that resources cannot be made available in sufficient amounts. Sometimes their difficulties are increased further by the presence of the category of 'special pupil' which Jones-Davies does not include – those with first languages other than English. His vision, however, is valid. Whereas he concludes his article – and has the last word in the book – with the assertion 'mixed-ability teaching is the quintessence of comprehensive education and as such must cater for all needs equally', it is our contention that its ease and feasibility in turn rests upon a prior condition of the truly comprehensive school – that it should receive a genuinely ability-balanced intake. But that must be a message to our political masters.

Brian Davies
Ronald G. Cave

1 Research findings on teaching groups in secondary schools

Peter Corbishley

'Research findings show' – a phrase that evinces mixed motives and emotions from teachers, not least when the topic researched is ability grouping. This, and other similar phrases, are used by some to establish a solid basis for teacher professionalism. To certain audiences, secure in their knowledge of research results, teachers claim to be trained specialists rightly knowing more than others, particularly parents. On more formal occasions, the phrases become personalized – Piaget tells us, Bernstein has shown – revealing teacher intimacy with the Great. But at other moments and to many teachers, such phrases become a threat, indications of teacher subordination and defencelessness. Research is then perceived as providing unjustified, unfair, unfounded criticisms of hard-worked practitioners. In this view, it is produced unceasingly by those in the ivory towers of Institutes, Councils and National Foundations.

Research also assumes different meanings for different generations of teachers. It can often be a powerful opiate which dulls and adjusts sensitivities to the routines of school or enhances them into fanciful imaginings. To the 'experienced old hand', findings reveal commonplace continuities; to the 'fresh and enthusiastic' real proof that schools can change to novel practices.

What is required is that teachers receive research less authoritatively and less subjectively. As a profession (not as individuals) they and not researchers still have the prime responsibility for directing, creating and maintaining pedagogies and pupil groupings.

It is also the case that specialist research reports are not (and may in principle never be) directly open to teachers. What follows is one attempt to enable teachers to come to grips with research reports. It is an attempt which relies initially on the idea that differences in findings may simply reflect differences between schools.

Differences exist in the ways in which in different countries, teaching different social mixes at the primary or secondary level, teachers produce individually different classroom situations. Arguments about some of these differences – in school organization, grouping, curriculum, teaching style – are often still little more than a distraction from how current practices create or characterize school systems which produce individuals who have different chances of reaching occupations unlike or similar to those of their parents. This is especially true about arguments on whether formal or informal teaching styles make for better learning.

The organization of research itself and the internal structures of life in those ivory towers has not helped, either, in enabling teachers to reach a more balanced view. Studies on school organization belong to the subject area of school administration. Those concerned with classroom climate belong to social psychology. Those concerned with the organization of knowledge for pupils are located in the sociology of educational knowledge. Educational research itself has recently become a topic area often separated from psychological or sociological studies of education, although educational researchers – and most of the studies on ability grouping – in the main continue to rely heavily on psychological or social psychological approaches. It may not be surprising, then, that from 1920 till 1974 well over 200 individuals, mostly in America, have conducted studies on grouping in schools. But the accumulated body of knowledge is minimal and very easily summarized.

1 Attainment as measured by standardized tests is not directly or consistently affected by variations in grouping practices, so that some studies favour streaming, some favour mixed ability and some are inconclusive.[1] Several suggest that grouping by itself is not enough; changes are also required in curricula, classroom organization, patterns of pupil work etc. I add the 'etc.' not out of conceptual laziness but because the list is seemingly endless. It is perhaps wise to add for an English audience that American studies, which in their general orientation were favourable to streaming and yet found little change of attainment consequent upon streaming, explained the 'failure' in terms of teachers' lack of adaptation of curricula etc. Teachers, it was upheld, simply failed to take advantage of the new grouping regime under analysis. This American reference should

underline for teachers in England that neither streaming, setting, banding or mixed ability are in any timeless or natural sense the only right, just and inevitable way of going about teaching pupils. Neither are they intrinsically easier or more difficult ways of doing so. Their acceptance depends on what other social and school features, whether recognized or unrecognized, are present.

2   The social effects of particular grouping practices vary across time and across national boundaries. They may also vary, although this cannot be checked, as between different regions within countries. For instance, in America in the period 1920-1935, research interested in proving the superiority of streaming for attainment, tended to find that streaming favoured students of average and below average ability without detriment to the performance of the bright. Similar results have also been found in English and Swedish studies for mixed-ability grouping for the period 1955-1964. The underlying argument is that both types of grouping are egalitarian. If personality tests are conducted, personal and social attitudes are found to be unaffected or positively affected by the social status patterns which either form of grouping is taken to imply. In the later period in America (1957-1964), streaming is found to favour the brightest without detriment to the performance of other pupils or of the sociability of all pupils. In England and Sweden in the same period, streaming is found to have detrimental consequences for low-stream pupils in terms of both performance, personality and attitude to the school.

If one neglects to break the research into periods and countries, this overall pattern disappears and there seem to be about as many pros as cons for any form of grouping. An alternative account could argue not that the results have been 'fiddled' to the researcher's own bias but rather that they reflect genuine differences. In America, in the early period, when mixed ability remained the norm in both elementary and public schools, any streaming attempted presupposed a social background which sought to reduce differences between pupils. It also presupposed teachers generally committed to a common education for all the newly arriving immigrants, and the flow was steady until it came to an abrupt halt in the 1920s. (The peak year for immigration into America was 1907.) In the later period, when the national need seemed to require an educational structure geared for competition with Russia, streaming again delivered the goods, in terms of attainment, but without detriment to the basic democratic ethic. It is significant that in the early 1960s, when the location for studies switched to schools where there were high numbers of negroes,[2] streaming produced effects very similar to those studied in England and Sweden for children from working-class backgrounds. Not surprisingly also, when studies are undertaken of schools trying for a comprehensive educational principle in times of some national concern for exploiting all levels of ability, as recently in Sweden and England, findings result which reflect successful implementation of a degree of equality in mixed-ability groups but without detriment to the attainment of the most able. It must also be added that the comprehensive principle may be a rather different animal in America (and English primary schools) than in the majority of English and Swedish secondary schools. Schools (for a particular age-range or over all ages) which are valued, in part, for their contribution in bringing pupils together (for creating a 'community'), will tend to be different from those of a society where schools are valued (not solely of course) for the efficient contribution they make to economic growth. In these respects, teachers, administrators and parents will also vary, whatever their nationality, in the value they place on schools, again leading to further local differences, which may be identified both geographically and socially. The differences indicated will only be evident at that local level. Overall, larger effects than grouping will contribute to failure or successes in schools, taken at a survey level.

3   The third 'finding' is that the teacher in the classroom is shown, or presented as, or inferred to be the crucial factor in determining the 'success' of any form of grouping. If teachers favour streaming, it works; if mixed ability, then that too works. This emphasis on teachers is not a recent one but is present in early reports. It is a persistent theme, unlike the interest in tests of the degree of social mixing in the classroom (usually by sociometric tests, increasingly used since 1934) or the concern for pupil self-concept (evident since the early 1950s, and which more recently has come to focus especially on the degree of anxiety felt by pupils). Strangely enough, important dimensions of the teacher variable have not been followed up. Just what is it that leads individual teachers to believe in a particular

4

form of grouping? And in change contexts are teachers effective only for an added range of pupils whose improved performance then contributes to a higher average performance for the class as a whole? No attention has likewise been paid to pupil attitudes and to the extent to which they wanted and would work for the particular forms of social and academic esteem offered by, or just otherwise available in a particular school.

4   My fourth point is not a finding as such but a more technical comment on the quality and presentation of the studies whose results have just been summarized.

It should already be clear that the results offered are not directly helpful to classroom teachers on whom successful implementation of change finally depends. To my mind, this is not in itself a criticism of research workers. It points to a lack in the organized procedures for disseminating and discussing research work. Given their limited time and money, the organization of such structures cannot lie with researchers themselves. The restriction of such procedures to the channels of publication of books or in journals itself suggests that no great value is to be placed on the results of research, except in so far as it legitimates policy (or research itself). Individual studies have often been used in this way to promote particular grouping structures. Further problems in the interpretation of studies immediately arise. There are no rules for knowing when a study is 'oriented' in the direction of a particular state of affairs. It is important to exclude those who may have 'fiddled' their results, whether this can be known or not, and I am not talking of deliberate attempts at falsification or bias on the part of researchers. A slant in emphasis is not likely to be a direct expression of the researcher's own values, although one can assume a general 'liberality' of opinion. The presentation of studies does, however, seem often to be affected by an anticipation of what will be deemed important in terms of policy. 'Results' which do not seem to have any obvious consequences within whatever is the current debate on policy are left unemphasized even when made available. In short, it is the very desire of researchers to prove themselves useful, that often leads to research results that 'fit' a particular viewpoint which may or may not be that of the authors, but is very likely to be that of administrators or policy makers. There are two evident causes for this form of over-emphasis. One lies externally in the processes by which research is funded; the second is internal and lies in the lack of general theories in educational research which could provide alternative controls of the presentation of results.

Instead, scientific technique is called upon to substitute for theory. Studies on grouping have been of two kinds. There are those which are surveys of existing practices, often designed to measure the spread of an innovation in grouping; and there are those which represent a move to controlled 'experimental' work. Educational researchers find their own explanation for the general inconclusiveness of their work by pointing to weaknesses in 'scientific method'. The argument that insufficient of the variables – curriculum, pedagogy, etc. – were controlled for, has already been mentioned. The earliest argument against survey work was, however, that it did not provide a control group for comparison with the primary research situation. But if one deliberately creates groups to experiment with, one is abstracting from normal school processes, especially from the possible effect of grouping over time. Experiments could fail to achieve worthwhile results, simply because the effects of grouping *are* cumulative over time. Yet, to set up experimental schools has not proved particularly feasible. The alternative of introducing certain standardized tests suffers from our inability to control all the relevant factors. Complications may arise because pupils work harder when they are the focus of special interest and attention rather than because they are grouped differently. Or the teachers, conscious of the research project, themselves vary their effort. Researchers tend to take the inherent limitations of a particular chosen technique as the source of the failure to produce significant results. They place their hopes on its improvement or correction. The alternative is to live with the inadequacy and try to balance out the pros and cons of each technique and arrive at an overarching conclusion independent of method as such. The need for a general theory then becomes apparent. The approach which combines survey and standardized testing tries to establish the generality of its conclusions by covering a large number of representative schools systematically. As an approach, it traditionally seems to combine the best effects of all approaches. It does, however, assume that schools are part of a system in which the features which make for differences are known and can be controlled for. The knowledge of what are significant features rests on previous work which contains the same basic assumptions: that schools are part and parcel of a functioning system, and that all schools have the same basic set of goals and aims. My own assumption is contrary. Schools can be viewed as idiosyncratic organizations which, within guidelines – which are most often and basically financial – respond to local, rather than general social features. Particular sets of pupils, born of particular parents, in schools organized by a local education authority, recruiting teachers at different stages of their career, makes for difference not similarity. Overall and in the long run, there are discernible trends, but these are predominantly the effect of social status and class hierarchy. These become active as reflected through the attitudes of teachers as a 'profession' with its own history and its peculiar career structures, as well as the attitudes of pupils, parents and local political figures (formed outside of schools).

Generally, patterns of school grouping are thought by teacher, pupils and others to play a part in social mobility. Researchers should not assume, however, that the labels streaming, mixed ability or whatever are the prime indicator of the realities at work. These names of themselves do not tell us enough of their meaning in the local context. It is not surprising, that over a large range of schools and a long period of time, the local differences indicated simply cancel each other out. We are left with an accumulation of results of minimal power. I will illustrate this abstract argument more concretely, but I hope to have also begun to clarify the notion that researchers are less likely to promote their own biases in writing up their work than to anticipate its contribution to policies of administrators which societally may be integration, economic efficiency or the life chances of pupils. A discipline which focuses on education in isolation from its local or national context inevitably gives itself over to lifeless generality. This leads to feelings that such research is irrelevant, especially among teachers who are not exempt from the fears which numbers and tables of numbers bring about. It is of prime importance in reading research to read such tables. Problems of value anticipation as outlined may be apparent in the way the problem is posed. More likely they are present in how the measurements presented in the text are put into words and which measurements are presented (for reasons of space not all results, etc. can be published), and whether they are presented numerically in tabular form or verbally (see, for example, Barker-Lunn 1970, Bennett 1976).

History

The form of ability grouping known as streaming was introduced in Detroit schools in 1920. It was called the XYZ plan, X marking the group of most able and Z that of the least able pupils. Five years previously, Detroit had introduced a scheme in which the most able pupils were separated from all others. The XYZ plan was therefore an extension of the process of 'topping' a group of pupils of its high ability levels. 'Creaming-off' has been reported as early as 1913 in a Liverpool elementary school. In America, such classes were known as Terman classes after the psychologist who had expressed a concern for preserving an aristocracy of talent, shaped to be leaders of society. Grouping by ability in the American context has always been taken to imply consequences for the shape and form of democracy. Terman wished to adapt the newly-developed procedures for measuring standardized intelligence to school organization, as outlined in the book he edited in 1924. In England, in that year, a government committee also recommended the adoption of standardized testing to facilitate transfer between schools and organization within schools. This recommendation was accepted in the Hadow Report of 1931 which proposed an ABC plan of grouping. From then on, in England, streaming gradually became accepted practice even in primary schools from age seven, well before the age of transfer. In America, in spite of publicity to the contrary, streaming has never become acceptable. This rather startling contrast requires further explanation. It also has far-reaching consequences of the kind already described, for interpretations of the results of research into ability grouping. Perhaps the most crucial point to emphasize, given current English attitudes to progressive education, is that streaming both here and in America was regarded as progressive.

In America, the banner was carried by psychologists working in education and by certain of the administrators, as in Detroit. Streaming, as a practice, was greatly encouraged by the advent of the testing procedures which were thought to determine IQ and ability with considerable reliability. It was advocated as a move to child-centredness, the argument being that by narrowing the ability range of a class the teacher is allowed greater opportunity to deal with individual learning problems. The association of streaming and child-centredness sounds strange to English ears, but it was a point emphasized by Hadow. 'Tracking', as that report calls it would enable the 'artificial' and 'conventional' classification of subjects to be broken down and related to the child's interests. In the following quotation (HMSO 1931, xxiii) the word 'stream' is used in a sense which also captures something of the sense of forward movement which the new method was to bring.

> The essential point is that the curriculum should not be loaded with inert ideas and crude blocks of facts, which are devoid of significance till related to some interest in the minds of the pupils. It must be vivid, realistic, a stream in motion, not a stagnant pool.

The naturalistic metaphor is indicative perhaps of a certain romanticism, but it is a metaphor which explains the English adoption of the word, 'streaming', as opposed to the more American term 'homogeneous grouping'. Christian Schiller (1963 TES) recalls the advice that a senior colleague in the Inspectorate gave to heads at the time of the Report.

> Find out what each boy and girl can do, sort them into classes accordingly, give each class the sort of work that interests them, and is within their powers, and let the class flow each year through the school like a stream.

Even though educationalists now regard the Report's recommendations of streaming as anomalous regarding the other contents and attitudes of its preface which are well known, streaming then was clearly part and parcel of the hopes of the English progressive educational establishment. At that time, English education had opted for secondary schooling on a selective scale. In America, they were committed to secondary education for all within a system which retained grading of the curriculum. Streaming, it was argued, was a logical extension to the efficient and scientific business management of schools then in vogue. It was to be judged in terms of its efficacy in promoting learning at the individual level, rather than generally weighed against mixed-ability or heterogeneous grouping. The technical difficulty for American educationalists was whether homogeneity on the basis of grouping was ever truly possible. As late as the mid-1940s, grouping plans were to be introduced which took the principle of streaming down to sub-groups within the classroom in an attempt to reach homogeneity. But it was still found that differences in rate and amount of learning persisted and were even variable for any given individual who, at one time, would work faster and at another slower, for no reason which could be solved by forms of class grouping. Streaming, then, in the American context did not favour individualization of learning. It was also opposed for its possible social division. The school was to be a melting-pot from which individuals could emerge by their own efforts.

In England, the technical problem did not lie in whether homogeneity of pupils was possible or desirable – those benefits were assumed – but rather in whether standardized tests or attainment tests should be used to group pupils, particularly at eleven plus. Which was most efficient? (Only later did the question also become 'and fair'?) Long before comprehensives were promoted as a solution, the dispute was over the accuracy of allocation at eleven plus particularly as it became clear in the 1950s that not all who passed the eleven plus went on to succeed at O level. Thus flow the studies of streaming in grammar schools, one of which will be looked at in detail. The emphasis within the studies on ability grouping here, and in America, reflects these assumptions on the problems which grouping regimes called forth and were thus required to meet. In one important sense, the studies themselves are the medium in which the respective debates were conducted. Thus from the 1920s onwards there are American articles on the harmful social consequences of streaming, on the importance of teacher attitudes and philosophy; and there is the early application of tests to measure sociability within classrooms. But these emphases are much later in the English work, as is the discovery of the social divisiveness associated with streaming.

Colin Lacey's study of Hightown Grammar[3] is a valuable addition to this history of grouping, as it provides a concrete account covering the same period (1904–1970) but also illustrates how at different times, the same school was different in terms of its clientele and how the grouping practices evolved to meet them. The evidence on grouping itself before 1950 is scanty, but certainly the picture in the 1960s is very clear and perhaps not untypical of other schools, for reasons which should become clearer below.

Until 1959, the school had created two express streams which enabled pupils to sit O level a year earlier than normal. This arrangement in turn, allowed a much smaller group of pupils to sit Oxbridge entrance examinations in the third year of the sixth form while still only eighteen plus. There is little evidence that the policy 'worked', but this was its overt rationale. In 1959, one of the express streams was dropped due, the headmaster claimed, to the failure of teachers to push pupils hard enough. It is clear from Lacey's data that the school was also receiving a lower and therefore much narrower range of ability at intake. (The school took in just over a third of the 300 eleven-plus 'passes'; 300 was 15 per cent of the junior leavers in 1956, but as the population declined this percentage increased.)

Streaming of whatever form took place at the beginning of the second year after a year of (diagnostic) mixed ability. A new head was appointed in 1963. A year later, he replaced streaming with a combination of mixed ability and setting by subject (where requested) which was introduced successively year by year. The rationale was that this was a response to the drop in the quality of the intake as measured by IQ. The overall consequence was a dramatic improvement in performance at O level together with a dispersal of the 'sink stream' effect created under the previous regime.

It would be inadequate to regard this as a natural experiment favouring mixed ability, even though other studies in grammar schools indicate similar if not such spectacular rises in achievement levels after a turn to mixed ability.

The interest of the changeover in grouping which Lacey happened upon, lies not in the contrast as such, but in the associated features of the historical and local context. His methods and mode of data presentation allow a reconceptualizing in some degree along these lines. Lacey himself structures his study by contrasting an early period (1904–1921) when pupils (and parents) treated Hightown Municipal Secondary School (as it was then) as a finishing school. Attendance at the school brought more favourable chances of superior employment. Examination success was marginal to the facility the school offered for jumping off into such jobs, if need be, before the end of the three-year course. In the later period (1946–1965 onwards) the attendance at the school provided the opportunity for examination successes which could lead to university degrees and access to jobs on the national scene. Lacey calls this 'the professionalizing' period. The interim period (1922–1945) he regards as transitional. Underlying this dichotomizing of time periods is Lacey's concern for access to educational opportunity. His analysis of the operation and effects of streaming for those in the lower stream (and of lower social class) is his central means of establishing inefficiencies. It may be for this reason that he studied a school which always – amounting at times to nearly a 100 per cent of the intake – recruited heavily from scholarship boys, rather than fee-payers. It may also explain why he emphasizes that the school, even in the 1960s, had a problem of retaining pupils at the upper levels. The problem of the early period of keeping pupils on for the full course had moved on to one of encouraging enough to stay on into the sixth form.

Neglecting Lacey's underlying interest in equality of opportunity I prefer, on the basis of another article,[4] to stay with the idea of 'retention', particularly as this notion emphasizes the status and social location of Hightown in relation to other local schools and to the local population. Lacey clearly adverts to this, providing the information that Hightown was located within a fairly stable working-class community in a suburban district, constantly losing middle-class parents through emigration from 1920 onwards. Such parents, Lacey surmises, would opt if possible for the more prestigious direct grant grammar schools. Lacey also notes, but given the lack of research into this topic cannot really comment upon, possible ramifications of the local grammar school provision for Roman Catholics. After the war, however, Hightown Grammar was more popular in parental eyes than the newly-created technical school which indeed moved into the old grammar school premises when Hightown moved into new premises in 1956.

Young and Brandis have suggested, with application to comprehensive schools, that superficially the same practice of streaming can refer to quite different educational realities. Conceptually, they suggest a link between more rigid streaming and a school geared to retaining bright working-class pupils, and an association between more fluid streaming and a clientele of lesser ability, but middle-class pupils. In the situation of retention where a school is attempting to isolate a sub-group of pupils from their 'mates' in the wider social context, they suggest that both teachers and pupils will value school organization for its capacity to deliver the goods. Commitment to school norms via assemblies, school clubs, houses, school teams, will be relatively low. Pupils in the lower streams will have less prestige, but can register that without loss of self-image. Studies which have reported no loss of self-concept among lower streams might well have been conducted in schools oriented instrumentally in much this sort of way to saving some pupils for 'education' by rigidly separating them from their peers.

In their suggested alternative polar type, a school could have a clientele of relatively less intelligent but more motivated middle-class children. Such pupils could be expected to accept the expressive mores of the school as relayed through assemblies and house teams. In this context, streaming would tend to render academic failure as personal and culpable. In order to show that work and effort are rewarded, transfer between streams would be made easier. This streaming would be less rigid and even replaced, given large enough schools, with banding. Their particular contrast has no direct foundation in Hightown, though it was a school where retention of middle- or working-class pupils was a perennial problem. As Brandis and Young use the term, retention implies the provision of education to those who would not otherwise receive it. Hightown's problems are historically more complex. It was unable to provide a five-year course of secondary education until 1922. At that point, most entrants entered on scholarships. Accommodation for the five-year course was initially provided by cutting the number of forms at entry. Access to education was simultaneously enlarged and reduced. But a 1944 type provision had in effect arrived some ten years before the school became a grammar in 1932. However, the effects of the depression led to the number of scholarship places being cut back to reduce public expenditure. Despite this, the working-class entry remained as before between 30 and 40 per cent of the intake. But its performance, compared with that of the lower middle-class, improved and its members stayed on longer. Economic circumstances (perhaps aided by the organization of an early form of the express stream?)[5] made for retention. Certainly the scholarship boys set themselves over the fee-payers.

After the war, the school was organized on the assumption that two of the four forms in any year would provide pupils suitable for Oxbridge entry. This division of the school, which largely coincided with social class, paralleled the earlier division between fee-payers and scholarships. Once again, a longer secondary education became associated with a middle-class background. The earlier situation of retention – common in several pre-war grammar schools – gives way to the picture outlined in several studies, especially those of Jackson, in which rigid streaming becomes associated directly with social class and in the case of the bottom stream disproportionately so. This is the situation which has been referred to as 'sponsorship'.

The new head entering the school in 1963 assumed that all pupils should be guided to good performance at O level and redistributed resources appropriately. He appeared to assume that successful retention could be taken for granted, and turned to the problem of motivating an intake of reduced ability by providing the more flexible scheme of mixed ability with setting, which led, in the years directly studied by Lacey, to an increase in all-round attainment. The research reports which suggest that mixed-ability grouping does increase personal involvement in both classwork and school might well have come from schools in this kind of context. Unfortunately, such reports do not give us the further information which would enable us to decide which of these patterns might be at work at this level.

The only inkling of comprehensive reorganization in Lacey's book comes over the resiting of the technical school on the same 'campus' as the grammar. At least parents of pupils at the grammar school took this as a preparation for the eventual union of the schools in one comprehensive. Generally in England, comprehensive reorganization has been sporadic. A national comprehensive system is unlikely before 1980. In Sweden, the changeover was smoother and earlier, coming in the 1950s. Extended secondary education for most pupils was a phenomenon of the 1920s in America. Significantly, interest in ability grouping, especially of a heterogeneous kind, waxes in these periods of the extension of secondary education to all below a certain age – often sixteen.

The societal pressures making for extended education are complex. Opinions differ as to the relative importance of push and pull factors in the economy, over and against cultural valuations of educational opportunity as a good thing. Thus one cannot talk of correspondences between societies and groupings without taking into consideration other forces and features of a local and national nature. It is for that reason that Yates's (1966, 1971) views are too simple or even simplistic,[6] in that if we assume that with comprehensivization and a degree of unstreaming, European countries are shifting to an American pattern of multiple elites, the form of mixed-ability grouping may still be different. Yates's analogy assumes a communalizing effect for mixed ability on the American pattern, but in the English context, it may be that mixed ability is valued mainly for the superior selection and more carefully sorted sponsorship it permits.[7]

Little has been said in this last section to allow the individual teacher room to recognize his or her own situation. The purpose has been to outline ways in which practising teachers can approach research reports so as to begin to formulate for themselves some of the notions and values which probably implicitly structure their classroom work. No review either has been made of the increasing number of articles and books which tell teachers 'how to do it'. In the main, that is not because individual contributions are not helpful. But these articles do suffer from a similar defect to many of the research reports referred to in the text, that is to say, inadequate description of the local features of any one classroom or grouping change. Recognition of relevant features by other teachers reading the articles is thereby made more difficult. Their own attempts thereby tend to be more tentative, more open to reversion and to effort which is misplaced because local circumstances are different.

Remembering that the various and contradictory findings may all have equal validity in so far as they objectify different educational and social realities – realities it must be added which are different in degree and not absolutely – two lessons may be drawn. One, is that researchers set in different disciplines must get together in order to make sensible comparisons possible. The second, is that while adequately conducted research can add breadth and depth to the necessarily limited local and practical experience of teachers, it is up to them to clarify their own policies and philosophies as to what they are doing and what the likely consequences may be. It is salutary then to remember that during the last great economic depression in this country, streaming was the progressive educational practice that was implemented.

Notes

1 As the latest review of the literature put it: 'The only general agreement about the results of research hitherto is that no agreement has been reached.' Morrison (1976), p. 1.
2 In this period, America faced up to integrating negroes. The Supreme Court pronounced upon the connection between streaming and racial segregation. Interest in research in streaming waned, except for studies documenting the link. Heterogeneous grouping within schools returned to favour. The neighbourhood base of schools was also challenged in the light of public recognition of the association between school catchment and housing areas. 'Bussing' has not been found to be a solution, given parental attitudes. 'Community' schools in England will face similar problems if administrative and political effort is not put into educating parents as well as giving them 'choice'.
3 The study published in 1970 (p. 193) ends: 'The general direction is clear. The major objective for those interested in increasing the supply of highly trained personnel from our schools must be the anti-group subcultures within secondary schools.' The undesirable social and academic consequences of streaming are located in terms of the efficiency of links between school and industry. The present 'Great Debate' seems centred on retaining this emphasis within comprehensive schools, and steering them away from the possible 'egalitarian' emphasis of some supporters of comprehensives. Mixed ability in such an emphasis is diagnostic – delaying selection until feasible. If accompanied by standardized tests at repeated intervals, two years of mixed ability combines the advantages of standardized and attainment tests without detriment to selection of examination course in the fourth - and fifth-years. Extensive pastoral care and close links with motivated parents from the local community should only improve the diagnosis. What is important is not to cheer on the terms but to take heed of the possible reality behind the vocabularies used. The study of Hightown as it destreams is available in Lacey (1974).
4 Young and Brandis (1967).
5 cf. Lacey (1970), pp. 23, 25, 188.
6 See for example p. 79 (1966), p. 95 (1971).
7 The term 'sponsorship' originates with Turner (1974). He suggests that social ascent via education is governed by different norms in different societies. The American system is characterized by 'contest' and the English by 'sponsored' mobility. American 'mixed ability' is valued for its promotion of formal equal contest, European streaming for its guarantee of early social selection.

References

BARKER-LUNN, J. C. (1970) *Streaming in the Primary School* NFER

BENNETT, N. (1976) *Teaching Style and Pupil Progress* Open Books

BOARD OF EDUCATION (GB) (1931) *Report on the Primary School* (W. H. Hadow) HMSO

LACEY, C. (1970) *Hightown Grammar* Manchester University Books

LACEY, C. (1974) 'Destreaming in a "pressured" academic environment' in J. Eggleston (ed) *Contemporary Research in the Sociology of Education* Methuen

MORRISON, C. M. (1976) *Ability Grouping and Mixed-Ability Grouping in Secondary Schools* The Scottish Council for Research in Education

TURNER, R. H. (1974) 'Sponsored and Contest Mobility and the School System' in R. Hopper (ed) *Reading in the Theory of Educational Systems* Hutchinson University Library

SCHILLER, C. (1963) *Times are Changing* TES Supplement 1 March

YOUNG, D. A., BRANDIS W. (1967) *Two Types of Streaming and Their Probable Application in Comprehensive Schools* University of London Institute of Education Bulletin New Series No. 11, pp. 13–16 Spring, or B. R. COSIN *et al* (eds) *School and Society*, pp. 149–151 Routledge and Kegan Paul/Open University

YATES, A. (1966) *Grouping in Education* John Wiley and Sons

YATES, A. (1971) *The Organization of Schooling: A Study of Educational Practices* Routledge and Kegan Paul

2 Meanings and motives in 'going mixed ability'

Brian Davies

'Going mixed ability' has become very much part of the working experience of a large number of secondary school teachers, particularly within the last five or six years. The move away from traditional teaching group arrangements has increased rapidly in association with secondary reorganization, though it did not begin with it. A decade ago most reorganizations did not involve much adoption of mixed-ability grouping. The comprehensive school, as was the case with its grammar, secondary modern and other elder brethren, tended simply to institutionalize the historic post-war orthodoxy about the efficiency of teaching to homogeneous ability/attainment groups. It streamed and where the size of intake merited it, banded, moving on to setting. Indeed, one was more likely to find the grammar or secondary modern school practising mixed ability within the confines of their ability range.

The grammar school variant was relatively uninteresting. The incursions of early choice to accommodate particularly second and third languages, usually *de facto* produced situations very similar to those which the explicit pursuit of streams or sets would bring about. The handful of secondary moderns that went mixed ability constituted very often a far more serious educational statement. Sometimes this sprang from a genuinely ideological commitment to the attempt to actualize a 'seamless garment' view of child ability and even, in some cases, knowledge too. Some few schools, under the same post-Newsom impulse which created courses like that led by Charity James and others at Goldsmith's College, sought what were, in terms of the practices of the secondary school past, radically different versions of grouping and curricular types. These sought to shake off the weight of apparently predestined relationships between measured abilities, teaching group membership and 'appropriate' differentiated curriculum. Few as they were, they swam dead against the tide pulling the secondary modern in the direction of public respectability (especially public examination access for as many as possible) so aptly described by Taylor.[1] By resisting early segregation by ability, by attempting curricular and pedagogical innovation and even more so by instituting 'levelling' policies like CSE-only entries, they frequently ran into difficulties both with parents and (with honourable exceptions) LEAs. Like so much local innovation in British education, most died rapidly with the departure (often for promotion) of their principal players. Some few became important sources of a diaspora of energetic individuals whose movement out into other schools, advisory roles and so forth can be traced even in an area as educationally complex as London.

Whereas the tales of most of the secondary modern mixed-ability innovators have remained largely unsung, a number of the comprehensive experiences are better known.[2] Many of these had the advantage of starting from scratch, or at least before the cast had really set. Some of these, too, like Countesthorpe, involved far-reaching curricular as well as grouping realignments. Others, like Woodlands, involved unusual, socially fascinating alterations in pastoral regimes. But the real growth in mixed-ability grouping matches the equally sharp rise in genuine reorganization of the last half decade.

This is certainly the case as revealed by research conducted by Peter Corbishley and myself in seventeen of the twenty-one Greater London Authorities during the period 1975–1976. Much of the data which I will call upon for subsequent argument is drawn from this SSRC funded work, which will be fully reported next year. Our survey, at the level of local authorities and schools, set out to discover which types of secondary schools were grouping in what sorts of ways in the school year 1974–5. Each school in all participating authorities provided a return as to grouping procedures for the 11–16 age range (with appropriate variation where middle school or other arrangements were found) which was matched against background data as to staffing, pupil intake, finance etc. gathered largely from local authority sources. In addition, socio-economic data for each authority was collected. Even more importantly, 12 per cent of the schools were visited in order to collect information via interview as to why the school (as represented usually by the head or director of studies) had chosen its current grouping and curricular policy.

On personal and public evidence, we have little grounds for believing that Greater London is untypical in terms of what has been happening in England and Wales at large. It does, after all, include a tremendous range of authorities as to size and socio-economic type from ILEA to tiny Kingston. Whereas the outer boroughs do have in common a shortish ancestry dating only from 1965, in educational terms they at the same time represent all shades of secondary re-organization (or lack of it). On the other hand, several of the LCC comprehensives inherited by ILEA have histories as long, relatively, as almost any in the country. At least the arguments may be taken as illustrative of what has been happening in some 500 schools in a vast conurbation. I am sure that they will ring true to a larger audience.

Who does it?

We must remember that schools go mixed ability within their own specific local authority context. Our rather naive research belief was that, given schools' – that is to say, headmasters, senior staff and departments – autonomy in respect of their choices of grouping practices, timetable and syllabus arrangements we would find a random incidence of grouping types over this large area. There is, of course, an important core of reality to the independence of individual schools within our system. But there is, at the same time, a striking non-randomness to the pattern, by frequency and type, of grouping arrangements in our schools by local authority divisions. Where re-organization is complete, it is possible to find cases of virtually ubiquitous first-year mixed ability, explicable only at the level of policy decision, formal or informal, at the authority level. These cases are probably rare and even when they exist, the odd school can still stand out against them. But it is perfectly common to find the best part of half the schools in reorganized or largely reorganized authorities having mixed-ability first years. In unreorganized authorities, the incidence is markedly lower. It tends to be confined to a minority of non-selective schools who frequently see going mixed ability as im-plicated in regenerating their standing in the pecking order engen-dered by relatively complex and subtle systems of residual parental choice.

A very significant proportion of schools that organize on mixed-ability lines in the first year, exempt or partially exempt, mathematics and modern languages from the arrangement, either from the start, or after a brief diagnostic period. We shall discuss some of the reasons offered for this below. Almost none attempt to carry on without explicit separate arrangements for remedial extraction or a remedial class, though the salience of this provision depends crucially upon the proportions of less-able children in their intake. A significant minority of schools within some authorities – and this may well be a growing tendency – 'top and tail' their intakes for grouping purposes, keeping a 'bright' as well as a remedial group outside of the 'mixed ability' arrangement.

In schools with first-year mixed ability, there are successive fall-offs in its pursuit into second- and third-years. The typical second-year pattern is not so much to abandon it but to allow firmer and more frequent exemptions by subjects from it, usually into setting. This often solidifies into third-year arrangements which in effect presage the banding of the fourth-, and fifth-years more than they resemble the commonality of the first.

A minority of schools are enthusiastic destreamers up to fourteen. These tend at one extreme to be schools with balanced or beneficently 'bright' intakes. Their initial successful experience, usually with first-year unstreaming, cumulates into a certainty that it is technically feasible in years two and three. At the other extreme, they are schools with depressed intakes where divisions would appear to be little more than an exercise in separating goats from goats. In this latter case, the 'one-band realism' is the same in kind as that which increasingly leads the selective school to delay homogeneous grouping for a year or two.

Though some schools would claim, in effect, to have mixed-ability groups in some fourth- and fifth-year curriculum areas, this is rarely the result of deliberate choice of best strategy. It is far more likely to be a limited *de facto* outcome of the relation between options on offer and pupil elections. Where numbers available entail the necessity of more than one teaching group, setting and differentiation by exam (or non-exam) destination almost invariably follows. Very many schools now exhibit at the surface an apparently complex, flexible and open system of choices for 15–16 year olds. There is no doubt that some schools do try very hard to institutionalize a lack of closure between children of all abilities and any given curriculum area. But the widespread reality is much simpler than this: core curriculum in the majority of schools *for the last two years* of compulsory attendance has shrunk to a highly attenuated minimum. English is the only sure feature. Mathematics is frequently not provided right across the ability and option ranges in non-grammar school fourth- and fifth-years. Some of the energy going into the current 'Great Debate' might well be expended upon asking 'why' concentrating particularly upon the relationships between specialist teacher shortage and pupil demotivation. God and the body are often dead. For the rest, the great fourth-year choice usually comes down to an election for one or other of linked blocks of subjects. At the extremes of the high status differentiated subjects – mathematics, the sciences, modern languages particularly – and the more practically oriented end – the design and workshop complex, domestic science, typewriting and commerce and ROSLA courses by any transmuted name – these represent as firmly a divided curriculum as ever existed under tripartism, and perhaps more so. This, at least, may be the real import of the constantly reiterated worry on the part of heads and others discovered during the course of our school visits as to the effect of increasingly ramified fourth- and fifth-year option systems upon 'core' curriculum. We found many anxious for a reversion to an extended core, while wanting to retain the real benefits of flexible choice as visited particularly upon those of above and average ability.

Mixed-ability grouping, then, particularly in the lower secondary (11–14) and middle school is very much with us. Its *meaning*, even in a basic sense, is of course somewhat problematic. To go mixed ability with a thoroughly unbalanced entry is a substantially different phenomenon to attempting it across the full range of child attainment, notwithstanding the maxim about 'all classes being mixed-ability'.

It has not been a notable feature of the British move toward the common secondary school to place the necessity of a balanced intake at the centre of the administrative and policy stage. Where this has been publicly pronounced, it has often run up against resistant pressures of geography and parental wishes. The politics of 'choice' has passed through an intriguing stage.[3] Never having effectively had it as a universal principle at secondary allocation – the 'choices' have long effectively hinged on having the income to opt out of the state system, passing the eleven plus or having effective claim to denominational status – in many authorities, introducing comprehensivization has given it a new edge. The scenario is familiar. The new comprehensive school *can* obviously be given a catchment area and an authority can be divided up more or less neatly into educational parishes (though this is certainly more difficult than appears, particularly in complex urban areas, given the historical growth and siting of school plant). But most comprehensives 'come from' somewhere, they have a previous and resistant former life as the ex-grammar, ex-secondary modern, ex-amalgamation of a number of schools, Moreover, their 'natural' catchment areas often point firmly to a neighborhood of one distinctive character or another. The run up to comprehensivization in an authority is likely to be politicized and exacerbated at the level of public debate. The fears of the 'middle-class' or 'informed' parent need to be assuaged. The answer comes back from officers and committee, 'let there be choice, over and above the rights of sibs and non-sinners'. In effect, let there be 'reserved places' and marketable places, let there be single-sex schools, particularly to allay the fear of disorder in the hearts of parents of girls, let there be schools specializing in the nurture of particular talents. The upshot can be complex to say the least, particularly in authorities blessed or cursed with 'spare places'. The parentally-shaken kaleidoscope, presided over by administrators bent on the quiet life can rapidly produce a hierarchy of comprehensives. They can range from the girls' grammar that has hardly lost one iota of tone, to the desperately depressed sink school with a largely press-ganged and numerically short intake, whose problems of morale are further devastated by long-term uncertainty as to the continuation of its very existence.

As we face a period of falling secondary school populations, all this will enter a potentially even more devious phase in which at the very least, decently built up comprehensives with no more than a manageable dearth of the more able, may find the intake-cargo shifting under their feet. The *modus operandi* of a school is forged, often painfully, over time with a given sort of child clientele. This is crucially the case in respect of the problems raised by mixed-ability grouping. 'Which secondary school will my child go to?' is a vital pressure point in our class and wider social system. We should watch the influences which play upon it very carefully. Man does not live by ability grouping alone but the meaning of ability grouping does depend upon intake.

What is mixed-ability grouping ?

No apologies need be made for treating this as an awkward and debateable question to be set against wider features of educational change. In a (straightforward) sense, the change to mixed ability is the easiest major innovation that a single person can accomplish within a secondary school. The hand that controls the timetable can, no doubt with considerable unwisdom, switch grouping practices overnight. If the headmaster near to the anecdotal hearts of DES/ATO mixed-ability course members referred to by Caulfield in a later chapter is, strictly speaking, apocryphal, he certainly has several close living relatives. At its worst, mixed-ability grouping can be an unwanted change forced by a head upon a whole staffroom for no reason better than that it accords with his current version of *avant gardism*, educational good faith or the right career vibes. There are plenty of schools where it has been pushed through at least to the sound of a studied staffroom silence or where the noise never penetrated the front office. In these situations, it tends to produce nothing but tokenism and subversion. Indeed, even in schools outwardly committed to the change, individual departments (particularly where basic teaching groups can be further subdivided on account of good staffing ratios, e.g. three forms as half of a mixed-ability year sent to science to meet four teachers) may make reversionary remixtures which heads either fail or do not want to notice.

Even granted relief from such problems, going mixed ability raises rather than solves questions of how children are effectively treated within classrooms. Unstreaming classes does not lead to 'unstreamed' teaching attitudes or practices. A teacher meeting a mixed-ability class may elect for any number of a variety of sub-grouping devices. He may attempt to continue 'wholeclass' teaching or he may begin the long preparative haul to as near possible individual treatment of each child. Most settle for some classroom grouping pattern that has as its cornerstone the bright, the average and the dull child duly conceptualized as presenting characteristic control and behaviour problems.

The recalcitrant mixer of abilities will not shift far. Much pedagogy and content choice settles – under-resourced and under-conceived – for appropriateness to the mass in the middle, with tops and bottoms considered to be harassing 'problems'.

It is necessary to get all this in perspective. We should be both amazed and awed at 'overnight' transformations – amazed at the total professional irresponsibility involved and awed by the sight of the problems facing teacher and taught. There is no doubt that in many schools, whole first years do get unstreamed after months of meeting and working parties where proselytizing or a politically central minority prevails over an unconvinced majority. Frequently, in these cases, neither will nor time allow for proper preparation as the vesting-day approaches, usually hedged by the possibility of 'fall-back' after a trial period, into setting or banding. Little new provision is made for resources and there is no organized staff retraining. This situation is *far* from apocryphal – one encounters it time and time again. We may call it Dunno or Ewantedit mixed ability after applying the following standard staffroom test question to a sample of incumbents: why are you doing it?

Teachers caught up in this sort of indecency may well be themselves partly to blame for its existence. Fear, self-interest, laziness and value commitment are all near cousins when really threatening change is in the offing. The head who comes to the point of exasperated insistence (Gentlemen, let us try it. . .) in the face of recalcitrant colleagues whose arguments for the *status quo* are no more powerful than 'you just can't do it with these kids' deserves some of our sympathy. But most must go to the teacher who, in most cases, is asked to make changes which go right to the heart of his practice and thinking in relation to children and knowledge. Moreover, in the present state (possibly any state) of educational knowledge, he will have likely heard no convincing argument as to why he should make this massive move. Almost everything is potentially out of kilter: at the end of the day, the change, if it is to be successful, must be carried out by individual teachers, sufficiently convinced and well-resourced. Instead he feels bullied and bereft, politically and theoretically unable to answer back.

All this is brand new. Whole-year-groups-almost-overnight mixing of ability, except in cases of new schools – where presumably congenial staff can be specially recruited – is a latter day educational perversion. It betokens how little we know about organizations and change in education. It is the bent reflection of other happenings. Before the recent wave, schools almost invariably went mixed ability by enthusiast and department. The change might fixate as an exotic bloom in an otherwise traditional school garden, even perhaps to be shown off with pride, but not pretty enough to become the envy of colleagues. On the other hand, it might spread year by year (timetable lumpiness permitting) from one department to another, with or without final prune for tidiness toward the end of the process. In an era of high staff turnover and general buoyancy of numbers and resources, departmental cross-fertilization could be rapidly engendered. Few mixed-ability traverses have been accomplished without strategic staff replacements, but at least all this entailed practice which did not violate the reality of a teacher, weakly trained with strong subject identities, unable to surmount the mental barrier of ingrained differences between children. Those unwilling to change could carry on or easily go.

The massive extension of the mixed-ability phenomenon seems to have been fuelled by the convergence of an insufficiently grasped understanding of the historic importance of the cross-fertilization process in earlier cases with a more than ample sense of guilt and dismay as to the bad effects of streaming. The context for the extension has been provided by reorganizations, actual or prospective. Amalgamations, extensions of ability ranges, new school creations all entail answering afresh vital questions as to what the purposes of a school are. New appointments, particularly to headships, sometimes the refurbishing of an advisory team, add to the organizational loosening ready for change. From then on, the mechanics can be all too seductive. The problem converts to 'what shall we do with our (new) intake?'

Mechanics and motives

To put the issue in this light is not to trivialize. Lower secondary school mixed ability comes at a very particular point in the eleven years of compulsory schooling which a child undergoes in our system. It has also become widespread at a particular point in the historic move toward reorganized mass education. The problems to which it must bear relationship within the careers of educands are those of performance and motivation. So far as the developing system is concerned, we might well suspect that it has something to do with the pursuit of either technical efficiency in selecting or altering the principles upon which selection is based in more egalitarian directions. In less high-flown but not simple terms, we must suspect that unstreaming is about deep-seated, perennial problems of the system. How do we manage and maximize children's performance? What constitutes fairness in so doing? Whose claims should we attend to most fully?

The suspicion should not lead us on to the belief that teachers and schools changing to mixed ability think about or think through their changing predominantly in these terms. We shall see below in more detail what patterns of attested motivations heads and the like offer. These do very frequently include general social, psychological, philosophical and political considerations. At the same time they are always set in the context of particular local circumstances. I would suggest, indeed, that these are in a major sense always uppermost. Schooling is statutory obligation: the show must go, on roofs provided over heads, local demography and community character met (freaks and all), the system (school and social) maintained. Dealing with an intake and dealing with society are not incompatible. Mixed ability may be adaptation to changing features of both, congenial to at least somebody's perception of the school's own needs in the system.

What do those who run schools say about their mixed ability? All have changed from or known something 'more traditional', so all expressed motives *for* tend to be prefaced by motives *against* something. Here, as with other educational innovations, educators tend to know more clearly what they are changing from, rather than changing to.

The great common denominator is a desire to get away from the worst features of streaming. These are most sharply focused upon as the production of demoralized, demotivated, unteachable middle-school groups, bad for themselves, their teachers and other children. A suburban near-balanced intake boys' school head put it succinctly: first and partial second-year mixed ability was adopted so as to 'avoid a rejected group because it would affect the work of the whole school and not just those kids'. He, no doubt, in common with the head of a comprehensive school with a rather more beleaguered and cosmopolitan past, wanted to avoid continuing a situation where 'band two curricula became a defeated area in terms of resources and staff interest which meant frustration for kids quite apart from the social stigma'. These sorts of sentiments tend to owe a great deal more to hard-won experience and a sensibility as to the real constraints and possibilities which hedge about schools, than to ideological fervour. They belong to people who tend to see comprehensive schools not as scenes for 'social juggling – education is more important than that' but as places where traditional rigidities are broken down. At the very least 'rigid streaming is not satisfactory because abilities vary from subject to subject' says a head, prefacing a claim to be aiming at a half-and-half mixture of mixed ability and setting in the lower school, over a five-year period. The pragmatic urges to get rid of sink-streams and improve child performances are of course indivisible.

Realism abounds and merges with perceptions of necessity. The newly-appointed deputy of another suburban school recently formed out of the amalgamation of two secondary moderns, sold short upon the authority's promise as to the new intake of able pupils, believed the new first year mixed-ability policy, 'was the headmaster's personal decision under forced circumstances. There was a lot of political upheaval when the schools came together, inter-staff bitching. He believed in mixed ability especially for the grey belt of dull-average kids who he thought could expand themselves in a mixed ability situation. . . . The headmistress of the girls' school became obstructive when it became known that the headmaster was to be appointed. There was a degree of anarchy with no hierarchy. They all came along in September and were presented with the new time-table and new posts and titles. The timetable had a first year mixed-ability regime with remedial extraction. Territory and power had to be fought out in the context of a timetable which was up the creek. One good maths teacher left because she thought mixed ability was all nonsense. . . .' Thus does a distinctive, but not unique reorganized school phoenix rise, in the words of a perceptive newcomer who has at least helped it to its knees.

While this degree of organizational beleaguerment may be un-common, dealing with feeder primaries is not. Sometimes the view is pretty definite. A very experienced head in a comprehensive with an intake strongly unbalanced towards the low-ability side thought, 'you can no longer rely on what in my time we called the mechanics of primary education. . . . That being so, I think that until they acquire the mechanics and come to see what they are being used for, it is rather wrong to label them in any special way on their arrival at school. . . .' This head felt that the failings of primary schools were sharpest for the least-able.

One of the great fears of somebody organizing schools is that they will find themselves with an uncontrollable population and certainly one's general discovery is that the least intelligent children tend to be more uncontrollable because the whole process of their education is a terrible strain and bores them. One is telling them to do something quite outside their competence so they know damn well they are going to be castigated for their performance and in the extreme case . . . they say 'well what the hell are exams for anyway because I really do not want to know about Boadicea, computers etc.' They want to be like their fathers or uncles or man down the street. To inspire in them the nobility of white collar work jobs is well nigh impossible anyway but they must smile at the attempts to do it. What the unstreamed situation does is to disguise the fact that the school is viewing any child in any different way from any other in regard to his future and it emphasizes the individual attention given to them. A chap who is finding it difficult in a mixed-ability group gets the attention he needs.

At the same time, he doesn't believe in just kidding children as to their abilities – like a neighbouring colleague he believes that 'kids can crack any codes you can devise'.

Even when views of the quality of the job done by primary schools are more neutral or favourable, real problems can remain. Many secondaries are fed by large numbers of primaries. There may be considerable differences in work schemes, grouping and pedagogical style between these schools and receiving secondaries may feel that a genuine moratorium, during which catching or evening up can take place, is necessary. This runs into two other factors. Secondaries frequently feel that they merely lack sufficient, reliable information from primaries, upon which they might properly base differentiated grouping. In some cases they also feel that 'settling in' is a difficulty for most children. A comprehensive head with only two feeders and a steadily improving ability intake, but with some fears about the geographical difficulties of getting to his school said: 'I believe very strongly in liaising with primary schools so I have been out and about meeting colleagues in our feeder primary schools arranging visits for myself and staff and vice versa during the normal school routine'. Open evenings for parents and visits for top juniors were also a feature. This same head believed 'that the mixed-ability approach for the first years is not a bad thing in lesson time because basically in the first year we see our task as helping the youngsters to feel at home and belong to their particular group – to give them some stability. They are going to teachers all over the place and moving around and this creates anxiety. So in some subjects, we keep mixed ability groups for lessons.' The groups being 'kept' were the basic pastoral form units. But mathematics, PE/games and craft were half-year setted even in the first year, after which flexible setting became the norm. The first years were thoroughly and repeatedly tested (and the programme moved up with them) via nationally standardized non-verbal, English and Arithmetic measures. To a great extent, this mixed ability was 'diagnostic' but in a context of a great deal of pastoral care and attention.

Other schools have more acute 'marketing' problems. Where parental choice of secondary school has any reality, these are automatically produced (one suspects that even if all schools were objectively equal parents would render them unequal). The school low down in the order of selection and wishing to rise must, in the language of the economist, indulge in backward, vertical integration toward the source of their raw materials. Connections with junior schools and parents take on a new edge as the traditional certitude of the child supply is tampered with. Public relations and public image have to abandon pomposity and reveal technical merit – good practice, seen to be done. Mixed-ability grouping can be offered in this sort of context as good design feature – a carefully planned strategy for assorting raw materials for the real business to come. It can be laid before parents (accompanied by appropriate topping and tailing, as required) as balm for aspiration which the system has cruelly turned into pretention by refusing their first choices.

These sorts of motives which are most typically offered, seem to belong very firmly to the longstanding preoccupation of British education: how to do differentiating better. They exhibit none of the levelling ideology which so stirs Black Paper and TES editors, merely a lower score on educational ritualism. But at their heart they are about diagnosis and efficiency. They are about both engendering sufficient child motivation so as to allow their talents to be managed *and* ensuring institutional survival in a world without the eleven plus. Funloving protagonists of child attainment competition should marvel everywhere. Red Riding Hood mixed ability lives kinder and more thorough than the examinatorial wolf: 'What a lot of mixed ability you've got in the first year, headmaster.' 'All the better to *set* them with, later, my child?' For once, an educational innovation offers to kill two birds with one stone. Time and again, heads reported immediate but sustained gains in child self-perceptions and attitudes to school, stemming from first-year destreaming. One cannot be quite sure whether this 'improvement in behaviour' syndrome flows from the mixed-ability change itself or other changes concomitant with it such as stabilization of pastoral groups or increase in teacher energies. One suspects that the initial improvement could hardly be maintained by the grouping change alone and can all too easily be dissipated in the absence of adjustment in content and pedagogy. Dispersing the baddies, though, has virtues which may be easily underestimated. The better attitudes – better behaviour – better work cycle which may be derived from the changeover working together with a number of other institutional pressures – from parents, for good public relations, from authorities and advisors, on account of poor messages from below, because of an extension of the ability range to be taught – that taken in conjunction with the power of the educational trendmill (change expands under pressure to fill any theoretical vacuum) we have the glimmerings of an explanation of mixed ability's spread.

The extension of the ability range to be taught – back to reorganization – completes the 'usual' pattern of motives. One might expect the common response to an extension of the ability range, given teacher and subject-centred pedagogy, to be along the lines of intensifying streaming, banding or setting. In many schools, this has been the straightforward answer to such change. Very often it is predicated on a dim or realistic view of teacher talents, admixed with the sharp end of the politics of amalgamation. Jobs and consultation are always the worried preface to going comprehensive. In how many amalgamations has unguarded difference in school status led to grammar school preferment, secondary modern dismay over appointments, and child and teacher apartheid in the bands? Unstreaming may act as a specific in this context too. Some heads value going mixed ability precisely because it means taking away from staff the opportunity to teach streams or bands. This can serve both to force teaching across the ability range upon everyone who operates in the lower school and putatively to increase thinking about, or attention to, the effective treatment of the whole of that range. While often stemming from deep dismay at the pariah-creating propensity of our streamed system (bright is beautiful), this impulse is also technicist in response. Indeed, it is sometimes couched pretty plainly in the language of production quality control: the managerial head may plan change explicitly so as to maximize his return (whether measurable or not) to any given set of inputs. A change to mixed ability here is akin to a basic change in school technology, which at least forces the teacher to do it *differently*. If one's view is like that of several heads we have encountered, that teachers have in the past tended to organize their work in relatively unthinking and minimal ways, then any change at least involves a fifty-fifty chance of improvement. The logic reads 'remove the traditional framework and they either get better or worse. The present is pretty bad for many kids, so we hope for the better.' Again in the recent past, teacher turnover could be hoped to do the rest.

Turnover of staff has been a tremendously important feature of the last two educational decades, peaking at Houghton and the subsequent demographic howlers. There is no doubt that if it could be kept in control by a head, it could change the character of a staffroom sharply within a couple of years. Out of control, of course, it effectively devolved power in a school to its stabler sub-parts. Schools with highest turnover have frequently also been the demographic transit-camps of our educational system, particularly in conurbations like London. There is hardly an authority or borough that does not have its unusually troubled establishments. Parents and pundits call them sink schools. Very often, at the bottom of their troubles, is demographic shift and administrative turn – or more precisely, in-decision. Socially, they are downtown, though it is amazing what this may mean relatively as between upper-middle class suburb and inner-city. Class and ethnic composition may be shifting, local authority housing policy may create them. The existence of spare places or indecision as to their future or continuance, can give them a tangible *Godot* quality. The sensible and often successful reaction of head and staff is to simplify some of the mechanics of school life. Either on account of the coming and going of child population term by term, or in prospect of a 'big change round the corner, though we don't know exactly when', mixed ability may be the answer, coupled with powerful pastoral intentions.

This case may presage an important future variant as more and more schools will become fixated, at least temporarily, at a permanent 'spare capacity' stage. Whether this be the case or not, such schools are sometimes reminiscent of the ethos of the secondary modern front-runners of the early sixties, except that they often operate under more extreme difficulties. But in a central ideological sense, they do, at times, get close to attempting to institutionalize not diagnostic or technical efficiency grouping and curricular types but genuinely 'communalizing' ones. These are the places which are sufficiently negligent as to schooling's manifestly differentiating task to send a Stuart Maclure mad with worry. They are numerically few and still distinctively heretical in professional terms. They can be genuinely keen on child interest, integrated (which usually means subject bits juxtaposed round a topic) content, group work and communal output. At best, they refuse to give up the vision of a genuinely sustained common curriculum. At worst, they are no more than classroom therapy supporting pastoral control whose real meaning is social rather than educational. They are schools that can excite the most paradoxical emotions: of delight that teachers' response to such socially and politically induced disaster can be so creative; of anger, at the odds which class and politics create, doubled for those who worry about them from a great height.

Schools who put their trust in Faith, Hirst and Charity in combination are sometimes found up the ability and social scale. They are more likely to have girl-only or denominational intakes or be ex-grammar schools than not. Their justifiers will speak the language of *Pygmalion in the Classroom* rather than the rugged populist tongue of the transit-camp secondary modern. Continuity and relative homogeneity of home/school values, plus a balanced intake, can produce a pastoral power and ease that makes space for grouping experiment. Change really is possible. They are good places to be – easy and supportive to teach in, bright and open to pupils, the pride of many a local authority's innovatory wing. They embody a vital message about successful educational change which is that *something* must be kept simple. Sometimes even, something has to be deliberately simplified or routinized in order to make space and release energy for the intended change itself. It takes considerable luck and talent to change successfully on several fronts. Going mixed ability is an enormous complexification for most teachers. These schools – they are the ones that tend to take it beyond the first year, to persevere with it in 'hard' curricular areas, to indulge only in remedial extraction and to sustain a broad core sometimes even beyond the third year – are often the antithesis of the downtowners in terms of the security they enjoy as to their successful past, ability intake and relations with parents and community. They have several vital advantages. They have energy for successful innovation. They foreshadow mass *education*.

The amazing thing about many schools in recent years has been the way in which innovation within them has been attempted simultaneously on many fronts. This state too often betokens the presence of that educational whizz kid, the ascending headmaster, sometimes with more bright literature in the head than fire in the belly or staying power in the tail. They can leave a devastated trail which imitators retrace even more disastrously. Even teacher-enthusiasts cannot take on changes in grouping, content and pedagogy simultaneously, without well-above average luck or talent. None of these changes can occur without at least a working conviction as to the validity of having a bash. The trade seems not to have noticed that early ability-mixers, where there was any real range of ability were happy as a first step *just* to mix. Changes in curriculum content and teaching techniques followed later, out of non-doctrinaire trial and error. We now almost automatically castigate the teacher unable or unreceptive to change on all of these fronts simultaneously. Yet we know that successfully institutionalized mixed-ability *teaching* is usually a painful, elective growth, more caught than taught.

Here lies the indicative rub: given the present state of the art, few schools can, or would justify their *going* mixed ability with reference to the known advantages of mixed-ability *teaching*. They sometimes revert from mixed-ability grouping because of the difficulty in making the traverse – lack of skill, resources or material having led to the new tyranny by endless amateur workcards. We know so little in a systematic way about timescales and patterns of success and failure.

Initially someone must plan and decide whether to go (who – head? whole staff? working party?). A decision must be taken by subjects or years, but in a very large number of schools no one, even of last year or the one before, can remember when the decision was taken. 'I can't say that there was a movement for change in the staff but they were receptive to ideas and prepared to listen and have a go . . . We went mixed ability in the midst of going comprehensive and "going mixed-ability" mixed in with curricular and other changes. So it was really done at various stages and various levels thus avoiding the crunch situation.' Someone has to get ready, arrange resources centrally/departmentally/individually if 'grouping' in any sense is to lead to 'teaching'. Enthusiasm and disillusion, losing or attracting staff will depend much upon initial consensus and working support. Reversion and revision is more common than spread and successful institutionalization.

To what effect ? Possible significance and outcomes
The question has a built-in overgenerality. What comes out depends upon what goes in and what goes in depends upon motives and resources (human and non-human). The very criteria used to allocate children to their mixed-ability teaching group are indicative of intentions and limitations upon outcomes. Extreme care with the even 'layering' of measured abilities within each group tends to go with diagnostic intention and short-run group/individual work programmes through which children can exhibit sufficient difference to be safely set or banded. Succumbing to additional criteria like experience of primary school French tends to be of a piece. Deliberate smashing up of junior school friendship groups/allegiances tends to operate as a subsidiary criterion. This is quite different from the deliberate dispersal of juniors with records of difficult or disruptive behaviour among a number of teaching groups, which is an ubiquitously claimed bonus. The more 'communalising' school will worry less about the precise mechanics of teaching group creation, will explicitly allow for friendships and sibs and will tend to organize the least able as if their lacks were genuinely remediable rather than fixed. This does not mean that they may not be filtered out into a separate group. They may be, but their treatment will tend to concentrate explicitly upon improving specific learning tools – especially reading – rather than upon purifying the remainder of their presence. Extraction will be more usual. Giving 'remedial' teachers the role of active assistance in preparing mainstream material for the

whole range is very rare, but is a sure index of a real common curriculum urge.

The real significances which we should look for are presumably in terms of what school is all about – managing knowledge and identity. We have not yet had the research which would enable us to say much about either. Among reigning intuitions, we must take seriously the noise that suggests that a move to mixed-ability teaching involves a possible narrowing and constriction of curriculum range. There are two dimensions. The first concerns the pressure which a mixed-ability commitment may exert upon the 'luxury' end of the curriculum, the minority preserve of the more able. The offering of second and third modern languages can come under pressure and the first (almost invariably French) may suffer loss of status. The position here though, is not nearly as clear as HMI appear to believe.[4] Where schools have mixed ability, French is normally organized immediately or early on into sets. We never have had a tradition of modern language teaching except to our education elite and even that has little historic depth. The malaise goes deeper than the injury done by the growth of mixed ability.

The more serious dimension applies to knowledge content in general. Our firm general impression, as earlier stated, is that content preparation tends to be dominated by a conception of three child audiences: the bright, average and dull. Preparation tends to converge toward the needs and abilities of the average. The bright are catered for by 'extra' or 'branching' work. To judge by the constant expression of guilt about how well this is done, there is a chronic problem here. But it is the pressure upon equity created by the condition of the less-able which may be more serious. They tend not to 'finish' lessons, topics or syllabus bits. If they do not finish, then to plan the next so as to presuppose mastery of what has preceded is to automatically disadvantage them further. But gains by the average and less-able, increases in their confidence and motivation, are part of usual intentions in going mixed-ability. The problem then is acute and sets up a strong presumption in favour of planning content, so as merely to juxtapose, rather than overlap conceptually cumulate topics.

The consequence for varying knowledge areas differs sharply. It offers a clue in part as to why English and the Humanities front-ran mixed-ability change: English has creativity; geography has regionality; and history has periods. Cumulation is unnecessary or displaced; events, topics, places are central. It should not surprise us either that the creative/workshop side of the curriculum should be thorough latter-day converts. But at the same time, we can see more clearly the difficulties of mathematics and modern languages. The difficulties of the latter are most acute. Meaningful gain without the qualitative transformation of material is difficult to engineer. Mathematics can manage for longer if there is disproportionate motivational gain. The science arguments in this area are now so varied and opposed, so far as the lower school is concerned, that success seems to hinge more on faith and choice of appropriate work scheme and support material than upon anything else. But even avid mixers cannot run French right down the ability range. Even where the less able go into 'French studies' two years' work at conventional pace takes three. Other gains coexist in terms of improvement in child self perceptions and delay in labelling. But even the production, so far as possible, of suitable 'mixed-ability' material has done less than in other difficult knowledge areas.

We have already made reference to what people believe mixed ability does to pupil identity and motivation. Again, we have no systematic research in this area as yet which is small scale enough to relate classroom events to child characteristics. In schools where grouping is groping we should expect regress as often as gain, of course. Where the change is seriously pursued into content and pedagogy we would expect loosening in the relation between ability and option choice and presumably increased long run attainment. Of the rest, for the moment, we should be silent.

Change within limits ?

Our understanding of change in education stands on a number of precarious footings. At a general level, it is easier to make out a more cogent case for educational practices as stabilisers, maintainers or resisters of social pressures than it is to show the converse. There *have* been times and societies when education has been used as the vital confirmatory tool of very great social and economic reorderings. But after the revolution, as well as in its absence, education above all repeats whatever passes for orthodoxy or ideological ascendance. It assorts, it transmits, it manages people and knowledge in relation to positions.

To grasp this, is not to be blinded by some cruel Machiavellian truth. There are plenty who would want to avert their gaze from it in a variety of other directions. Those who talk on glibly about education as assuring the development of potential or providing competitive open opportunity to be grasped, are as blinkered as those who locate the possibility of class warfare and renewal within educational relationships.[5] In the former case, there is an under-estimation of the social – class, cultural and economic – constraints, in the latter, often a doomed sense of over-determination. At least in this second instance, there is a proper grasping of the political (in its widest sense) implications of education. But the diagnosis is simply shallow. Education is not free to engineer rapid social change. It is only licensed to leaven, our social, cultural and political mix, to be fair within limits.

It does have on offer the one thing which is often frankly despised by those most intent on big-scale social change – differentiated knowing. We have got to the point in our changing system where the practical problem for educators is, in my view, how to maximize its availability to children.[6]

By what process are children of various sorts and conditions hooked on to lots of things worth knowing? Most teachers would settle for the fact that if this could be successfully located and institutionalized, society would insist upon doing the rest of the job anyway. What is more, it would be a task transformed. Ignorance is a show-stopping form of powerlessness. Teachers increasingly grasp that the proper use to which our school system's slender autonomy ought to be put, is to resist the mechanical power of allotting child actors to their traditional character parts. The altruistic bit of the mixed-ability move is school's contribution to society's growing unwillingness to categorize pejoratively.

It is all too easy for the Right and Left to denigrate this search for open education, the balanced curriculum, and varied and appropriate teaching methods. They can point to the shifts and turns of our educational past and present to see the bad that feeds their case. One side tends all too easily to lay the blame on child, home and educational trendmill; the other blames class, work relations and the State. Meanwhile, somewhere between the rowdy poles, schools change – albeit in a way very often more reminiscent of being overtaken by events than of leading them. But surely we can grasp this as a somewhat necessary general truth about educational systems? Given the task of reproduction and maintenance would we not expect them to have this rather uneasy relationship with change?

If this analysis is at all correct, it should redouble our wish to grasp the significance of our practices, difficult though that is. The organizational device of mixed-ability grouping is not a simple, uniform phenomenon. It serves several possible ends, setting up very different practical problems, in differing schools. In each and every one it needs to be asked 'why are we doing it?' and 'what is it doing?' as serious and separate questions. Somewhere among the answers there may be some modest clues as to how we bring about more abundant knowing.

Notes

1 See Taylor (1963). In his summing up he says 'whilst the modern school finds it difficult to provide education of the quality increasingly demanded, its position in the educational structure encourages the multiplicity of examination work and external signs of success.' (p. 162)
2 See, for example, Watts (1977 ed.) on Countesthorpe and Bernbaum (1972); Rowe (1971) on David Lister and Thompson (1970) on Woodlands.
3 See Stephens (1974), writing on some of these issues as Chief Education Officer of the London Borough of Waltham Forest.
4 See DES (1977).
5 For differing reasons, Cox and Dyson (1971) and subsequent fulminations at near yearly intervals. See especially Lynn, R. 'Streaming: Standards and Equality' in Goodbye Mr Short. *Black Paper* 3, 26–29, Critical Quarterly Society and Young and Whitty (1977) are equally clear about the danger of most 'progressivism', including mixed ability.
6 See Davies (1976).

References

BENN, C. and SIMON, B. (1970, 1972) *Half Way There* McGraw Hill (2nd ed) and Penguin

BERNBAUM, G. (1972) Countesthorpe College in *Case Studies in Educational Innovation: II, At the Regional Level* OECD

COX, C. B. and DYSON, A. E. (1971) *Black Papers on Education, One* Davis-Poynter (Critical Quarterly Society, all numbers to date)

DAVIES, B. (1976) *Social Control and Education* Methuen

DEPARTMENT OF EDUCATION AND SCIENCE (1977) *Maths, Science and Modern Languages in Maintained Schools in England. An Appraisal of Problems in Some Key Subjects by Her Majesty's Inspectorate*

FERRI, E. (1971) *Streaming – Two Years Later* NFER

ILEA INSPECTORATE SURVEY (1976) *Mixed-Ability Grouping* ILEA

JAMES, C. (1968) *Young Lives at Stake* Collins

BARKER-LUNN, J. (1970) *Streaming in Primary Schools* NFER

MONKS, T. G. (1968) *Comprehensive Education* NFER

MONKS, T. G. (1970) *Comprehensive Education in Action* NFER

ROSENTHAL, R. and JACOBSON, L. (1968) *Pygmalion in the Classroom* Holt, Rinehart Winston

ROWE, A. (1971) *School as a Guidance Community* Pearson

STEPHENS, W. E. D. (1974) Some are more equal than other *Times Educational Supplement* 17 April

TAYLOR, W. (1963) *The Secondary Modern School* Faber

THOMPSON, D. (1970) 'The Woodlands School, Coventry' in Halsall E. (ed) *Becoming Comprehensive: Case Histories* Pergamon

WATTS, J. (ed) (1977) *The Countesthorpe Experience. The First Five Years* Allen and Unwin

YOUNG, M. and WHITTY, G. (1977) Introduction: Perspectives on Education and Society in *Society, State and Schooling* The Falmer Press, 1–15

3 Planning for mixed ability

Bob Gough and Jimmy McGhee

Materials for Planning the Curriculum Unit, Schools Council

It is not the purpose of this chapter to present the philosophical or ideological arguments for or against mixed-ability grouping, but there is a need to examine the motivations and the mechanisms for the initial decision to unstream (or not to stream) since the strength and the origin of the reasons involved will tend to influence the kinds of patterns that emerge, and will also place limits on the extent to which teachers will put up with difficulties.

If a school staff freely, and with consensus, enters into an arrangement of mixed-ability groups because it is felt that a streaming system produces self-fulfilling prophesies of failure for some children, it may be anticipated that they will be concerned to design and produce resources appropriate to the different interests and abilities of their classes. If, on the other hand, a school staff has a system imposed on them by a head-teacher for some vague and ill-defined reason, one is not surprised when they respond with a defensive, coping strategy, i.e. they will adjust their present practice as little as is necessary in order to 'get by'. Such a response is by no means inevitable, and it may well be the case that such an imposition upon a passive – or even unwilling – staff, might force an examination of the issues involved, and this process could lead to procedures no less effective than if 'mixed ability' had been adopted by acclaim. The taking of the particular decision, in short, could be the necessary spur to 'concentrating the mind wonderfully'. In general, though, such a style of decision-making would not be recommended.

Whatever the reasons, and whatever their origin, for embracing the notion of mixed-ability grouping, there are two key issues which arise: (a) by what criteria are the pupils to be placed into groups, and (b) what changes – if any – will take place in classroom practice to deal with the changes in the nature of the population. This latter emphasizes the distinction that needs to be made between mixed-ability *grouping* and mixed-ability *teaching*.

To consider mixed-ability grouping first, one thing that needs clarification here is which abilities are being mixed? In a streaming system, children are often taught in groups which are based upon some supposed measure of 'ability', e.g., an IQ test. Sometimes the 'streams' (for all subjects) are based upon attainment in, say, Mathematics or English. We did encounter one secondary school in which the first year was streamed on the basis of primary French. Sometimes the criteria are so idiosyncratic as to defy categorization, and often they are accepted uncritically, if not unquestioningly, by some teachers. A teacher of French who had previously received children in 'English' sets ('setting' for us is one kind of streaming, and we would not distinguish it for the purpose of this chapter) claimed his job was going to be impossible if he received 'maths' sets. The teacher of PE, of course, has always had mixed-ability groups. Even if the pupils are grouped according to their attainment in the particular subject being taught, it may still be argued that *every* class is a mixed-ability class, in that it is highly unlikely that every child is working at the same pace, absorbing the same material with the same efficiency, and making the same sense of what is presented. (And indeed many teachers in streamed classes design their work to cater for the different capabilities and interests of their pupils.)

Another question is *how* mixed are the abilities, i.e., what is the nature of the school population? There will be differences between schools arising from their location, involving such things as the stage of secondary reorganization, the presence in the vicinity of selective schools, as well as those differences associated with socio-economic features. School A, for example, may have in its intake a very wide range of ability and may seek to form groups, each one of which reflects this spectrum. To do this, either access to something like IQ scores, or the administering of such tests by the school itself, is required. There are problems here about the adequacy of the testing, as well as about the validity of the test itself, and the groups so formed should not be expected to be precisely comparable in performance. If wide differences do emerge, however, it might encourage the teachers to examine their practices, rather than assume that such differences are explicable in terms of inherent qualities of pupils. (When a class is supposedly homogeneous in ability, teachers tend to differentiate between pupils on the basis of other criteria, e.g., 'behaviour' or 'attitude', or even politeness. When a class is by definition heterogeneous, the teacher now legitimately has an additional basis for differentiation, and the different application of this and the other criteria will tend to produce differences between groups.)

School B may find that the ability range of a particular year group may be encompassed by, say, some fifteen IQ points, and may constitute a skewed distribution with perhaps a high proportion of the pupils in the lower-ability ranges. A 'mixed-ability' class in a school like this is different from one in School A, and consequently poses different problems for the teacher. A 'mixed-ability' group in School B would clearly not be an 'all-ability' group. Where a school has a relatively small range of ability in its population and forms a 'remedial' group and, as happens sometimes, an accelerated group – 'topping and tailing' – one is led to ask questions about how 'mixed' are the groups in the middle, and how different this is from streaming.

Some schools make no attempt to obtain the whole range of ability available in each group. Some of these claim that since the main reasons for wishing to have mixed-ability groups are social ones, the ability range is not so important and the pupils can be allocated randomly to groups. (This is not of course 'random' in the statistical sense – but haphazard.) This may be done on the basis of initial letter of surname, or friendship, or kinship, or address, or some amalgam of these. Such groups are rarely comparable to population, owing to various biases in the procedures used.

The mechanism used by a school to allocate pupils to different groups will – as suggested above – tend to reflect the underlying philosophies prevailing in the school, although it may indeed run counter to the manifest, stated reasons for mixed-ability grouping. This may be made particularly evident by the way in which the extremes of the ability range – particularly perhaps the less-able – are treated. Is there a remedial group formed such that some of the children have special (and perhaps specially designated) teachers for most of time for a curriculum experience different in content, emphasis and pacing – even if sometimes masquerading as the same curriculum experience? Or is there a process of 'withdrawal' or 'remedial extraction' whereby small numbers of pupils are taken out of the normal timetable for special work on 'basic subjects'? Each of these devices poses problems. The formation of a remedial group tends to negate some of the claimed benefits of mixed-ability grouping, and in addition raises the issue whether there ought to be similar special treatment for the most able – and hence back into a streaming system. The extraction method requires planning in order to ascertain from which lessons the pupils are to be withdrawn. Is it always from the same lessons, or does it vary from week to week? In any event how is the equation made between the gain of the pupil in attending the remedial class, and his loss of attainment through not being at the lesson from which he is withdrawn? Further, is the remediation to be concerned only with reading, writing and simple numeracy, or are remedial science, remedial geography etc. to be included? Remedial extraction therefore requires careful planning if it is not to degenerate into a series of more-or-less *ad hoc* social occasions which contribute little to the deficiency in attainment for which the pupil was deemed remedial. This planning might take place within the context of a *remedial department* which could consist of a group of teachers especially recruited for the purpose of devoting attention to less-able pupils – in or out of mixed-ability contexts. Alternatively, a group of teachers could have a part-time commitment to remedial work, but such an arrangement needs systematic coordination. There are clearly implications here for such things as loyalty to departments, and for consultation and decision-making structures. Without adequate planning, remedial extraction may easily become a misguided, albeit benevolent activity, which fails to remedy anything, and may in fact produce new problems.

In some schools, the matter is made more complex by an additional system of allocation to groups for pastoral purposes. This is not the place to consider all of the ramifications of pastoral care systems. Sufficient to say that there are many ways of putting pupils into things like house groups, varying from an anonymous, haphazard allocation, to very complicated procedures involving kinship, friendship groups etc. Some schools go to great lengths to see that their pastoral groups also contain the whole of the ability range (where the pastoral groups are also in age groups) but, in these cases, it is difficult to see why pastoral groups should differ from teaching groups (other than perhaps in size).

Once mixed-ability groups have been established, the teacher has to consider what changes – if any – are necessary or desirable in pedagogy and in the content of the curriculum. (There are implications as well, of course, for evaluation procedures. This aspect is discussed more fully in chapter six by Rory Deale.) When visiting schools which have already introduced mixed-ability grouping, what one should perhaps look for is to what extent the classroom behaviour of the teachers (and of the pupils) differs from that of streamed classes. One needs to ask to what extent *ought* it to be different, and why, and whether it ought to be different all of the time? Again, responses to these questions are to some degree influenced by the motivations for grouping the pupils in this way. Has it been imposed on a reluctant staff, who might well adjust minimally to cope with their perceptions of the problem? Is it seen as a device for alleviating some of the social and behavioural problems of the school? – and in which case, is the teacher's focus on aspects of *control?* Or is it seen as part of a complex whole involving a relationship with the school's overall objectives? Here, some positive *educational* (rather than purely social) benefit might be attributed to, say, the involvement of pupils of differing ability simultaneously exploring certain concepts at various levels.

The central problem facing the teacher is that of providing a variety of resources to suit all levels of ability. The difficulties involved become more apparent at the extremes of the ability range, i.e., the problems of extending the most able, whilst at the same time giving enough attention and encouragement to the less able. Given the realization that mixed-ability teaching requires changes in the teacher's role, it is clear that the provision of resources in adequate quantity and of an appropriate nature is seen by teachers as the most important factor in achieving effective mixed-ability teaching. There are three main approaches to this:

1 Individualized material for each pupil.
2 Different material for different groups of pupils.
3 The same material for all pupils.

1 *Individualized* – this term has become debased by its too frequent use in contexts in which it is not entirely appropriate. We shall use 'individualized' to refer to a complex process by which a pupil's abilities, needs, interests etc. are diagnosed, and a unique programme of activity designed to cater for him is produced. This

variety of *independent* learning requires to be distinguished from that in which a group of pupils are all doing the same thing – e.g. responding to the same assignment card, even if it has been reproduced for their personal use. (This we might term *individuated*.) The criterion of pupils working by themselves is not a sufficient one to be labelled as individualized.

The growth of educational technology in the recent past has led, *inter alia*, to some interest being shown in schools towards individualized programmes. Many schools, moving towards mixed-ability grouping, see the use of these as a way of dealing with a wide-ability range. Some would argue that the use of such programmes means that you are not teaching 'mixed-ability' groups, but teaching individuals. In addition, such a practice would seem to be inconsistent with a view of teaching and learning that laid stress on the social context of the classroom as the medium in which pupils make sense of their world. The teacher's response to suggestions like these will again depend to some extent upon the reasons for which mixed-ability grouping was undertaken. But, in any case, individualization is a practice equally available in principle whether streaming or setting procedures are employed or not. If it is considered an appropriate mode of teaching and learning, then it is appropriate regardless of the kinds of grouping employed. Some teachers divide the curriculum into those aspects amenable to individualization – or to which an individualized approach might be considered necessary – and those aspects which may, in their view, be more profitably explored by other means. This may be particularly applicable in mixed-ability contexts.

A discussion of the difficulties posed by, and the advantages claimed for individualized programmes is beyond the scope of this chapter. What needs careful examination, however, is the notion that any teacher can scribble down assignments *ad lib* ('Every teacher an author'); can produce these as adequate assignment cards ('Every teacher a graphic designer'); at different levels to cope with the varying intellectual and linguistic capabilities of the pupils ('Every teacher a diagnostician') . . . satisfying the criteria involved in programmed learning ('Every teacher an educational technologist'). The issues which arise here are, anyway, appropriate problems for *all* teachers, but which have been made salient by the presence of mixed-ability grouping. A change to individualization *need* not involve any change in the content of curricula (although this is clearly possible), but will obviously be reflected in a change in pedagogy.

2 *Different material for different groups* – this implies a stratification of the pupils and a stratification of curriculum content, which are then matched. This could lead to what is virtually streaming within the classroom (and the acceptability of this will depend upon the motives for unstreaming in the first place). There are clearly problems here involving criteria for distinguishing between pupils and for distinguishing between levels of curriculum material. The pupils need to be presented with teaching material at different levels and one would expect their assignments to be different. The mode of operation in the classroom would obviously involve group work. This could entail different aspects of some topic, or theme being differently explored. (It could, indeed, take the form of quite separate, perhaps unrelated, activities for each group, but this would seem appropriate only where the availability of resources makes it necessary.) Again, the conceptual content of the curriculum need not be affected, although this is a possibility.

3 *The same material for all pupils* – different pupils interact with material in different ways, and this may become more evident when a group contains within it a wide range of ability. If the same curriculum material is offered, and the same assignments set, then differential outcomes should be anticipated. Those adopting this practice may argue the validity of exposing the pupils to the same experiences, exploring the same ideas and yet being aware of different responses and at different levels. In selecting material for inclusion in the curriculum, such teachers may be influenced in choosing things which are relatively easily 'teachable' in this context, and this might mean that some important areas are neglected.

A teacher will not necessarily confine himself to any one of these three approaches, and his unique school context will influence which particular mixture is seen as most appropriate. It is likely that the nature of the teacher's planning and preparation will have to change. It could mean a re-examination of the curriculum content he uses, and is likely to lead to a reappraisal of methods of approach. A teacher will find himself using a whole range of techniques (as effective teachers have always done). Although occasional 'class-teaching' should by no means be ruled out, pupils working in small groups is likely to be a common occurrence. To cater for the needs of these groups in his class usually involves the use of resources of a different nature from the kind of textbooks usually employed – and many teachers find themselves inexorably on an 'assignment-card' treadmill.

Some of the issues involved here have already been touched on. There are real problems to be considered regarding the quality of teacher-produced assignments, especially when they have to be produced by the teacher working alone, with little time, with little or no ancillary help, with inadequate resource provision etc. One of the main problems arises from the sheer volume of such material that seems necessary in order to cater for the wide and differing needs of the pupils. It is evident that teachers require assistance in this situation, and that some of this could be in the form of appropriate in-service education and training. This should, among other things, offer access to the whole range of alternative strategies available for mixed-ability teaching; help develop the skill and knowledge required to produce appropriate assignment cards (and indicate also the resource provision at local level necessary to achieve this); provide examples from the practice of other teachers which will serve to elucidate the issues more clearly; and provide facilities for cooperation such that through a division of labour and/or sharing of experience, some of the teacher's precious time can be saved.

These activities – and particularly the cooperation – could (and should) start within the school itself. There may well be people in the school with significant contributions to make, in terms of the way they deal with pupils, which might have particular relevance for a school moving towards mixed ability. However, the use of such people should not constitute the only in-service work undertaken, and should in any case be organized as part of a coherent programme designed to suit the vagaries and the needs of the particular school. Elements of such a programme should be directed specifically (although not entirely) towards two particular groups of teachers: those who have not reached the realization that mixed-ability teaching *is* an issue, and worthy of examination and those who will have to live with the consequences of the decision-making, but have not been involved in the discussions leading up to the decision. This may be the case, for example, either when a teacher chooses not to take part in the preliminary activity for some reason, or when a decision to have mixed-ability groups in the first two years of a secondary school is made by senior members of staff (head, deputies, heads of departments) none of whom will, in fact, be teaching any of the pupils concerned.

This leads us in to the important area of the management of innovations within a school. Some aspects have already been touched on incidentally, in terms of the reasons why mixed ability is considered, and the relationship between these and how it is manifested in practice. There are further questions to be raised concerning the people involved. Who is initiating the discussion? Is it the head teacher, or the senior staff as determined by departmental or faculty heads? Or is it a relatively junior member of staff, with lots of enthusiasm and energy, but not much credibility and not much power? Who supports and who is hostile to the idea? And are these stances related to the potential gains and losses as experienced by them? Which pupils are involved? Is it to apply throughout the school? If unstreaming stops at some stage, when is this, and why? Will all subjects be taught in mixed-ability groups? What are the criteria for exemption, and who decides? The general movement towards non-selection at eleven plus, and the increased incidence of mixed-ability groups in the first years of secondary schools are perhaps more than coincidental. It would seem the case that, in the wake of abolition of selection at the end of the primary school phase, there is a wide acceptance of the view that to select children (via streaming procedures) at the beginning of the secondary school phase would be inappropriate. Indeed, many – though not all – teachers see non-streamed classes as a logical development of comprehensivization. Thus, the introduction of mixed-ability grouping into the first year of a school is less of an issue than many other proposed innovations, and it may well be the case that teachers can continue (i.e. get by) without significant changes in their approach. It is when the extension of mixed-ability grouping into the second year is considered that it may, in fact, be a more significant change. The need to adopt alternative strategies and practices could be more demonstrable by this time. More attention is likely to be given to the difficulties involved in assessment and evaluation, depending upon the particular curricular pattern employed by the school in the third year. If the mixed-ability groups are to be retained, then there will perhaps need to be some procedure for selection of fourth- and fifth-year courses. If not, and some kind of setting or banding or streaming is to return in the third year, then the criteria (and the mechanism) for the allocation of pupils to different groups will have to be worked out.

In some large schools, with well-developed faculty structures, there may be other complications in that the timetabling may be such as to allow faculties to be autonomous in how they allocate pupils to groups. There is a possibility then of a range of different practices with little knowledge about them outside the particular faculty in which they are employed (and perhaps not a lot inside it!). It is by no means certain that in their allocation, faculties will use the information about the pupils that are available to the institution as a whole. Some teachers would argue the need for a consistent policy throughout a school regarding allocation to groups. At the least, it would seem important that everyone should be aware of the methods used in various parts of the same establishment. The possession of such autonomy by faculties may have a particular relevance for the organization of fourth- and fifth-year courses.

A deliberate policy of mixed-ability grouping is rarely found beyond the third year in secondary schools. In any case, it can be argued that such an arrangement with fourth- and fifth-year classes would tend to be of a different nature from non-streaming further down the school. Indeed, it is possible to find schools with an apparent 'mixed-ability' option system in the fourth and fifth years, following on from a streamed lower school (i.e. years 1, 2 and 3). Whereas in discussion of mixed ability re first-year pupils, 'ability' seems to imply some kind of general ability (sometimes labelled 'intelligence' or 'brightness') and 'mixed' tends to mean a deliberate policy formulated to produce the whole range of ability within each group, with fourth years the focus seems to be upon abilities which are relatively specific and concerned with attainment in particular curriculum areas, whilst 'mixed' tends to imply merely the absence of streaming, i.e. there are no formal arrangements for obtaining a spectrum, or otherwise, of ability in each group. Thus, the usual practice in secondary schools is to arrange for fourth- and fifth-year pupils a set of compulsory subjects – usually mathematics, English, physical education and religious education – together with some optional courses, the choice from which is more-or-less limited. The pupil-choice (sometimes 'guided' by a process of 'counselling') is influenced by restrictions placed upon access by various factors, e.g. the number of teachers available, their assessment of the merit of pupils who opt, the perceived need for a 'balance' of subjects etc. An apparently 'open' system of choice can produce an upper school in which some subject options are highly academic, examination-oriented (and hence of high status), whilst others are seen almost as remedial subjects. A spectrum of ability in each option course is unlikely to be produced incidentally by such a process, and any school which rates as important the formation of mixed-ability groups having this range must plan its procedures for allocation with great care, since 'chance' is unlikely to cater for their requirements.

This demonstrates once again the need for a school to have a very clear understanding of its reasons for wishing to have mixed-ability groups. It points also to the need for determining priorities, and even perhaps hierarchies of aims and objectives – namely the relative importance of a spectrum of ability in each group as compared with the desire for pupil choice. There are many teachers who consider mixed ability not to be an issue with fourth- and fifth-year pupils (even if it be so in the lower school) and require only the establishment of a system which does not inherently exclude any pupil from opting for a particular subject. Such teachers are aware that some options will recruit pupils from a markedly different ability range from others, but they will accept this, and even perhaps deem it appropriate. Thus, 'mixed-ability' grouping it may be, 'all-ability' it is unlikely to be, and – if it needs a label – perhaps just 'unstreamed' might be the most appropriate description.

However, there are some schools which deliberately seek to achieve teaching groups in their fourth and fifth year, which contain the whole ability range. Where this is the case, it is likely to reflect deeply-held convictions about the kinds of knowledge that ought to be made accessible to all pupils, and the logic of this would seem to imply the development of a fatter common core, with open access to a small number of options. There are questions which arise then about the nature of the common core. There seem to be several different meanings in current use of both 'common core' and 'common curriculum', and some discussion of this may be pertinent. 'Common core' tends to be used to refer to either:

1 a delineated set of knowledge/skills/activities considered as essential for all pupils. Thus, for each subject area, there may be a 'core' element together with a range of options with variable access.

or

2 a specifically-designed course (e.g. 'Social Education', 'Communication Skills') which every pupil must take.

This may take the form of a number of short courses more-or-less related. It might be more useful to refer to this variant as 'common *course*'.

'Common Curriculum' takes three broad forms, and as outlined here, what is common becomes respectively less.

1 All pupils are exposed to the same curriculum material in the same way and at the same pace.
2 All pupils are exposed to the same ideas, but these are presented in different ways to suit their different abilities and interests.
3 All pupils have the same subject labels on their timetables, but different offerings are made to different groups of pupils, selection for which is made within the department: obviously types 2 and 3 could involve some kind of banding/setting/streaming.

(Even where mixed-ability grouping is not seen as either appropriate or possible in the fourth and fifth year, some kind of common core/ common curriculum is still possible, of course, but not germane to this book.)

Much of the discussion about common core has been limited to notions about the inclusion or exclusion of certain subject areas. As the above treatment might suggest, unless attention is devoted to what is done within those subject areas in classrooms (and what is common about it) then such discussion could easily become fruitless.

Whether the mixed-ability grouping under consideration is a tentative introduction on an experimental basis in the first year, or an extension to other pupils, or a massive switch in arrangements, a lot of planning is necessary. As a first step, many schools arrange a day or half-day conference, at which teachers from schools which have already some experience of mixed ability are invited to talk about it. The usual pattern is that these talks are followed by questions and/or discussions in small groups. These discussions are often unstructured, or inadequately structured, in part, because the speakers may be brought from such distances as to make detailed advanced planning very difficult.

When a school has gone to a great deal of trouble – perhaps even involving a half-day closure, and the consequent negotiation with the local authority – to arrange such a conference, there is a great temptation to bring in as many different speakers as possible. By and large, this is counterproductive. There is a great deal of benefit to be gained by the staff of a school collectively being given the opportunity to stand aside from the day-to-day pressures of their teaching task – a rare enough event – and to use this breathing space to reflect upon themselves and their practice. To make the use of such an opportunity as effective as possible requires careful and detailed planning. This should not perhaps be directed at producing a procession of guest speakers from elsewhere, but should be devoted to identifying and clarifying the issues insofar as they affect *that particular school*, and to explore the teachers' responses to those issues.

It seems appropriate therefore to plan some activities before and after the conference, as well as the conference time itself. This three-stage process will then allow each of the many and varied facets of the matter to be explored in the most useful way. For example, if a school which has had mixed-ability grouping in its first year for some time is now considering a possible extension to the second year, then the pre-conference period could usefully be concerned with the careful and detailed gathering and analysis of information from those who have had experience with the first-year pupils. The conference itself might consider what differences it will make in second-year classes, and for whom, and the implications of these. Meetings after the conference might then cover detailed planning *vis-à-vis* the resources needed to deal with the new situation, and also with the wider and more long-term implications of the change, e.g. what is to happen in the third year? What about option choices in the fourth and fifth years? Will these be affected? And, of course, the necessary matter of *evaluation*: namely, how will you know that you have achieved what you set out to do; and what results constitute a valid educational experience for the pupils? (or at least no less valid than the previous practice!)

Descriptions of what has happened in other schools could be confined to written material in the form of case-studies of mixed ability teaching, and the presentation of such accounts could be given by the personnel concerned in the context of the external provision of in-service education (for example, at a Teachers' Centre), where a more general account of what is involved may not be inappropriate. Such a presentation does not replace the gain from a visit to a school which has made some progress, but it may supplement it. Personnel brought in from outside for any of the stages need to be recruited on the basis of their ability to make a useful contribution in terms of the specific context of that school, and an awareness of that context seems an important prerequisite. A local authority adviser, in some cases, is well placed to do this. This kind of 'school-based' (i.e. *school-focused* and largely *school-located*) activity has its inherent weaknesses (as well as its strengths). Amongst them are the dangers of introspection, of taking too narrow a view, and hence making assumptions about possible alternatives available which may be inadequately founded. Some of these may be attenuated by the incorporation into the planning of someone appropriate to act as a *consultant*, whose task would be to monitor the discussions, indicating inconsistencies, inadequacies, etc. The phrase 'critical friend', has been coined for such a role, and the person concerned should be a neutral, but caring, outsider with knowledge of the educational world in both its practical and theoretical aspects. He/she must of course be acceptable (and credible) as far as the school is concerned, and personal knowledge or recommendation may well be the only way to find such people. The local College of Education or Polytechnic or University may be a fruitful source, perhaps via teaching practice relationships.

In part due to the many and complex pressures on teachers, much change in our schools proceeds in a piecemeal, *ad hoc*, and often inadequately thought-out fashion. Effective mixed-ability teaching is very difficult and very taxing, in that it makes severe mental (and physical) demands upon the teachers concerned. Perhaps some of this can be alleviated, perhaps the demands will at least seem worthwhile if the decision to move towards mixed ability and the consequent practice arise from a coherent process of planning. It is in this belief that this chapter is offered.

4 Mixed-ability teaching at Hounslow Manor School

John White

Background information

Hounslow Manor was in September 1976 a group twelve school with ninety points, full-time teaching staff of ninety (including two on an Immigrant Project) plus one and a half part-time equivalents. Ancillary staff amounted to five and a half full-time equivalent clerical, one full-time librarian, one full-time technician, one full-time laboratory assistant plus two and a half full-time equivalent in term-time only. The school was nine form entry (268 intake in 1976), with boys and girls in nearly equal balance. There were 150 in the sixth form. The school estimated that it had sixty-six backward readers (defined as having a RA below nine years), with about one quarter of the intake receiving extra help. Children with English as a second language amount to about a quarter of the intake (but are not identical to those receiving remedial help). *Editors*

Hounslow Manor School, which is situated in the London Borough of Hounslow close to Heathrow Airport, was established in September 1968 as a six-form entry mixed comprehensive school for pupils aged 11–19. Previously the site was occupied by two small single sex secondary modern schools and very little additional building was required for the new school. The head teacher of the girls' school was appointed to the headship of the new comprehensive and I was appointed as deputy head, most of the staff being recruited from the original schools.

The school was organized with a vertical pastoral care system based on four houses, each of which had a head of house and eight house tutors. Each tutor group consisted of approximately twenty-five pupils of all ages and abilities. The academic work operated

E

within a banded system, an upper and lower band (which included a remedial department) and each subject department operated independently, coordination being arranged by either the head teacher or myself. In 1970 the Education Committee decided to increase the size of the school to eight-form entry (it has continued as nine to date) and in April 1974 the head teacher retired and I was appointed in her place.

During the intervening years, various developments had taken place including the establishment of heads of houses as above-scale posts; the introduction of directors of studies as senior posts and the operation of an option system for fourth- and fifth-year pupils. The school had enjoyed a good reputation and could feel that a successful start had been made in the field of comprehensive education.

However, by the time of my appointment as head teacher it was becoming increasingly obvious that if this success was to continue changes were necessary. The implementation of ROSLA, the continuation of the grammar schools in the area and the serious lack of a balanced ability intake into the school (7 to 8 per cent of high ability pupils represents about the most we have ever received) and the rapid growth in numbers of pupils and staff as well as buildings meant that the organization needed a complete reappraisal. There are few times in any school's history when it has the resources to meet its needs but by a combination of good fortune and judicious planning by my predecessor this was such a moment. A review of the school's establishment of above-scale posts, combined with a series of new appointments meant that not only was it possible to create the structure that would facilitate changes, but also, and even more important, such changes would be sufficiently supported and monitored so as to increase greatly their chance of success.

Setting up the machinery
I had three deputies (two have since achieved headships):

1 *first deputy pastoral* – responsible for all pastoral care arrangements and the day to day running of the school. Assisted by heads and deputies of houses, tutors and, recently,
2 *second deputy administration* – responsible for all aspects of school administration – assisted by the administrative officer and ancillary staff.

3 *second master curriculum* – responsible for the curriculum. Assisted by Directors of Studies (lower, middle, sixth year and remedial) careers director, faculty heads, heads of department and a resource coordinator. This latter newly created post proved crucial to the introduction of mixed-ability teaching.

In order to achieve the maximum consultation and coordination a complex committee structure was created as follows:

School Coordinating Committee – membership included the Senior Staff (4) Heads of Houses (4) Directors of Studies, Resources and Careers (6). This was later extended to include faculty heads (3) and a representative of the Curriculum Committee (1). This Committee first met in November 1974 and now meets once a fortnight after school under the chairmanship of the head teacher and is the major policy making committee, together with the staff meeting.

Curriculum Committee – this committee took over from the old Heads of Department meeting. Membership included all above (18) plus Heads and Sub-Heads of Department (21). This Committee meets three times a term under the Chairmanship of the Second Master (Curriculum) and deals with all curriculum matters. Curriculum Committee meetings are always followed by Departmental meetings.

Academic Board – membership is based on Faculties and Departments with Senior Staff as ex-officio. It first met in May 1974 and now meets at least six times a year, usually more often, and its terms of reference include the following:

(a) to provide a forum for reviewing the academic programme and determining examination policy
(b) to review, and where necessary promote, schemes of curriculum development, new courses and course integration
(c) to advise on capitation distribution
(d) to promote links with other educational institutions.

Not surprisingly the Academic Board has proved to be a pace-setter for curriculum development including the introduction of mixed-ability teaching.

Various other Committees have also been established such as the

School Services, School Council, Sixth Form Academic plus a number of sub-committees and working parties.

Each house staff meets once a week partly during school time and a weekly sheet is issued containing information for both staff and pupils. In addition, there are separate meetings of the heads of houses with the Senior Staff; and Directors of Studies, Resources and Careers with the Senior Staff, both mettings being held weekly in school time.

Through this interlocking structure it is possible (all committees are 'open' and minutes are published) for each staff member to be fully informed and consulted. Each post of responsibility (whether above-scale or not) has its published terms of reference and thus no responsibility is seen in isolation.

Each member of staff is supplied with a resources handbook (in addition to the staff handbook, staff diary and markbook and time-table handbook) which lists all the resource facilities available. These include a complete recording service for both TV and radio, a list of all available A/V equipment, and a fully staffed reprographic service for typing, duplicating and photocopying. These are based on the reprographics room and provide an immediate service to all staff. In addition courses are held every year in the use of all A/V and re-prographic equipment so that staff may operate the machines them-selves should they wish. All materials are supplied 'free', the cost being allocated from the school capitation. This was a deliberate policy decision and avoids a complicated accounting structure to produce the right charge on departments for materials used and means that no junior member of a department has to plead his case for materials for worksheets etc.

Moving away from upper and lower bands

By 1974 it was becoming increasingly obvious that our system of upper and lower banding of pupils was running into considerable difficulty. These two bands were composed of pupils from all four houses and within the bands classes were of mixed ability although there was some setting (e.g. mathematics). Pupils were placed in the upper or lower band according to information provided by primary schools. As Hounslow Education Committee permits an unrestricted choice of non-selective school to parents, pupils come into the first year from some thirty primary schools of very diverse nature. Approximately 25 per cent of our pupils are from the Indian sub-continent or East Africa, many of these having experienced considerable language problems in the primary schools. Sometimes one mark decided which band a pupil should be in and the situation was further complicated by the lower band including two remedial groups in the first year, which were to be discontinued in the second year as we wished to switch to a withdrawal system. These pupils had followed a separate curriculum in the first year. There was a real problem about absorbing them into ordinary band two classes in the second year.

Over the years the school had devised a system for changing pupils from one band to another. In theory, this could be arranged at any time at the request of staff but in practice, the final decision always remained with the appropriate head of house. Inevitably, this meant far more promotions than relegations and by the time the third year was reached band one classes were 'overflowing' and many band two classes had a definite 'sink' attachment to them. Some band two mathematics sets performed better than band one, modern languages in band two operated under grave difficulties and finally the operation of a free choice option scheme in the fourth year tended to create even more confusion, particularly when it became necessary to apply arbitrary rulings as regards eligibility for classes.

The decision was thus taken that in September 1974 the first-year intake would be divided into ten unstreamed groups and timetabled according to house (two houses to each house band), thus replacing the upper and lower band arrangements. The decision was preceded by very full discussion through all the Committees. In retrospect, it would be difficult (and possibly fruitless) to say at what precise point in time we made the decision about mixed ability. Certainly, the fact that we did arrive at it, rested in part on a number of complex and interlocking factors. We approached the subject cautiously and at great length. Our reasonably well-established consultative and communication systems meant that we avoided a front office – rest of staff split. I knew the staff well (having been deputy head for five and a half years previously) and I think that they had reasonable confidence in me. My second master (curriculum) provided a great deal of the driving force behind the mixed-ability innovation. Curiously enough, his experiences in a highly selective school convinced him that whenever you draw 'ability' lines you are likely to make mistakes and that pupils perform to the level of staff expectations. He was also concerned that by the time band two pupils had reached the third year, they presented considerable disciplinary problems. As I indicate below, our organization was complex enough to permit departmental blocking which allowed the potential 'fall back' of individual departments to decide upon forms of grouping.

The initial decision to proceed in the first year only was made for a variety of reasons. It was obvious to us all that if any change was to be made, it would be better to start with the pupils coming into the school. There was a better chance of getting an even spread of ability amongst the pupils within the houses, and therefore the study groups, although the shortage of able pupils and the fact that many pupils had brothers and sisters in the school and requested the same houses tended to complicate arrangements. Perhaps most decisive was the view that if the arrangement was to succeed it would necessitate much planning, extra care with staffing and the allocation of a considerable amount of resources. By dividing the year into two bands – not now upper and lower but in the sense of timetable blocks based on mixed-ability houses, with five teaching groups in each, class sizes were kept to twenty-seven and an additional member of staff was allocated to each English teaching block, thus giving twelve groups each of twenty-two/twenty-three pupils for this subject. The appointment of a resources coordinator meant full support from the A/V and reprographic services. Part of the capitation had been set aside for curriculum development and each department was encouraged to 'bid' particularly for assistance with the first-year work (the Academic Board made the recommendations for additional monies). By this means, the modern language department (since joined with the English department as part of the faculty of language) acquired the Longman's A/V course, and the English, humanities and mathematics department were able to purchase additional material. The science department (since joined with mathematics within one faculty) was able to strengthen its Nuffield combined science course. Wherever possible, staff who wished to visit schools or gain in-service training for mixed-ability work were released. The humanities department, which had the additional complication of initiating an integrated course for the first time in the first year, had staff released regularly in school time so that the work could be better planned and coordinated. A new head of humanities had been one of my first appointments as head teacher and the decision about an integrated course had been a departmental one.

As a 'fall back' situation, so as to allow for a degree of setting as well as regular extraction, certain subjects were blocked i.e. English, mathematics, and modern languages, and despite an uncertain start, due largely to an intake which contained an unfortunately large proportion of pupils with a reading age of less than nine, the system got under way. By Christmas 1974, the date by which decisions for the following year's timetable are finalized, reports from departments spoke encouragingly of the experiment.

Indeed, in my report to the school governors at the end of the 1974–5 school year I was able to state:

The programme has on the whole been successful. Departments have recorded a satisfactory first year of implementation and are pleased with the range of work produced and the way in which children of all abilities have continually applied themselves. There have also been significantly fewer discipline problems within study groups. This measure of success can be attributed to a number of inter-related issues. Perhaps most important was the thoroughness of preparation by staff. Each syllabus was carefully examined and adjusted and in many cases coordinated with work by other departments. Monitoring of exercise books in the major subjects illustrated the success of individual work. At the end of the year pupils who had entered the school with high junior school scores (closed tests) were sent for. They presented exercise books in all subjects covering a year's work. This reinforced the conclusion that mixed-ability teaching need not reduce or hamper the level at which these pupils are capable. Indeed, their output of work was impressive and the quality constant and of a high standard. Staff, however, are naturally cautious in their optimism. The time measure of success for the mixed-ability programme must lie in the future; not to be judged in one year. The following years will demonstrate just how much of this year's success has been due to the vigour and enthusiasm of the staff in preparation.

Meanwhile Committee meetings throughout the autumn term 1974 were much occupied by discussions concerning mixed-ability teaching.

Should the experiment be continued into the second year and if so, what effect would this have on the third and subsequent years? The two main areas of difficulty were the third year, whose pupils had had two years of the old system, and the English and mathematics classes in the fifth year, where, although setting could replace the banding arrangements, a move to new house bands would mean some disturbance to the groups which were half way through their CSE or O level courses. These subjects were raised at the September academic board meeting, when the second master in charge of curriculum matters suggested fourth- and fifth-year change. He prepared further information for the November meeting, where he also explained the effects of a house banding change on the next year's third year. The matters were further discussed at the subsequent January meeting. Meanwhile, the Curriculum Committee discussed and agreed the changes in principle in December. A special staff meeting to discuss arrangements was also held in this month.

It was finally agreed to continue the first-year change into the second and as considerable study group changes normally occur between the second and third year and later years, to switch completely to a house banding system for all years one to five in place of the upper and lower band arrangements. I think that the decisive point in the house banding argument was that house banding and blocking in year three and for mathematics and English in years four and five would permit each department to choose between broad setting and mixed ability, whereas the previous upper and lower banding arrangements ruled out this choice.

In order that all staff and pupils would understand the changes and the ideas behind them, two memoranda were issued: one to tutors in order for them to explain the new arrangements to all the pupils and the other to all staff setting out the rearrangements in more detail. The matter was also discussed fully by the School Council. Pupils' fears were mainly voiced by the able pupils as to whether the system would work. Would they be held back? They were also concerned that the new house banding arrangements would separate them from their friends. In addition a letter was sent to parents explaining these new arrangements.

The memoranda were as follows:

Memorandum 1 – tutor's guide to new banding arrangements
From September next (1975) a new banding system will be in operation. Pupils will no longer be placed in an upper or lower band according to ability, as this proved unsatisfactory in the past for many reasons, notably pupils in band two have felt themselves labelled as less successful and have lost heart. A number of pupils have been moved into band one but teachers have been very unwilling to sanction moves into band two, which has led to oversized classes in band one and great inflexibility resulting in difficulty in fitting pupils into their correct group.

In future, pupils will be placed in one of two house bands – yellow/green or red/blue. This division is solely in order to enable a timetable to be constructed which will offer the greatest possible flexibility. The aim is to enable departments to decide individually how they wish to group their pupils for lesson purposes, whether in sets of similar ability, or mixed-ability groups.

Broadly, for next year's second year the faculties of mathematics/ science and humanities have chosen to construct sets of similar ability to study their subjects, which means that once a child has been placed in his set, any change of set would mean a change of his timetable in all these subjects. The remaining subjects have chosen mixed-ability groupings for years one and two. As many of these subjects will be blocked (i.e. up to the five study groups of that year and house band will have the same time), it will be possible to reorganize the groups as ability sets, if this were thought desirable, without disrupting the rest of the timetable, as pupils could easily be moved from one group to another without their groupings for other subjects being affected.

In years four and five there will *normally* be two classes running simultaneously in any option subject, to enable setting where desirable, and blocking for compulsory subjects.

The banding change will cause the most disruption to the present second-year pupils who will be reorganized into different house study groups and may therefore resent separation from friends in other house groups. However some changes normally take place at the end of the second year and the change to fourth-year options causes further separation from friends and so they are simply suffering a year earlier than usual. The educational gains should well outweigh the social disturbance.

NB A separate more detailed sheet concerning timetable arrangements for 1975–76 will also be available.

Memorandum II – timetable arrangements for 1975/76
Information for staff

In September 1974, the last year intake was divided into ten unstreamed groups and timetabled according to house. Five groups from red and blue houses followed one timetable and five from yellow and green followed another. This system replaced a division into two timetables based on upper and lower ability determined from information provided by the junior schools.

Proposals for 1975/76

Next year it is proposed to continue house banding into year two and to phase out what remains of the former ability banding system, i.e. in years three, four and five. This means that the somewhat inflexible band one and band two division can be replaced by setting arrangements on a departmental or faculty basis within each house band.

Implementation

Year 1 As for 74–75, with additional blocking arrangements for mathematics and English to allow three classes for each house, i.e. twelve groups altogether.

Year 2 Continuation of mixed-ability groups for English, modern languages and creative arts – blocking arrangements for upper and lower-ability sets in mathematics, science and humanities – blocking arrangements for teaching boys and girls craft and games in house bands.

Year 3 The present second year pupils will need to be redistributed according to house. There will be separate timetables for red/blue and yellow/green. English, mathematics and humanities will have separate blocking arrangements to allow setting. Craft and games are blocked in House bands. All other subjects appear in option blocks which are sufficiently flexible to allow pupils to be *directed* into courses according to ability and suitability.

Year 4 The option arrangements are substantially the same as for 1974/75 but with pairing arrangements to allow setting in *most* subjects. All other studies will be taught according to house bands. In particular English and mathematics will be in red/blue or yellow/green groups and blocked to allow setting.

Year 5 Identical options to 1974–75 for year 4. However the present fourth-year groups for mathematics, English and religious studies will need to be redistributed according to house. The blocking arrangements will continue to allow setting but *only within the house bands*.

Year 6 The option programme for the lower sixth will allow choices from five independent option blocks of six periods each. The blocks contain subjects at all levels to accommodate pupils of differing abilities.

Conclusion

Subject to staffing, the new proposals are feasible in terms of timetable structure and provide a considerable degree of flexibility with regard to setting within departments. This will mean that class sizes can be controlled more easily and that pupils can be redistributed within the subject if necessary. The long term advantages may be said to outweigh the unavoidable short term effects of redistributing the present second-year pupils.

(NB In the event it was possible to have only ten and not twelve mathematics groups in year one.)

Consolidating the change

For the current timetable (1976–77) both science and humanities have chosen to continue mixed-ability teaching throughout the second year, leaving mathematics the only 'broad setted' subject. Modern languages may commence broad setting half way through the year, although the increased interest in this subject has resulted in far more students being recommended by staff to continue with a second modern language in the third year. Mixed-ability classes continue in English until the fourth year.

Staff interest in the curriculum has increased tremendously. A detailed monitoring of attainment, effort and attendance for each subject was proposed (by a faculty head) at an Academic Board meeting. This has developed into three curriculum checks for each pupil each year. Staff provided grades (A to E for attainment, $+2$ to -2 for diligence, A to C for attendance) for each pupil taking their subject. These are collated by Directors of Studies and a pilot scheme involving a separate curriculum record card for each pupil is being undertaken at the moment (autumn term 1976). Each house will have a nominated curriculum coordinator who will be responsible for recording each pupil's performance in his house and obtaining supplementary information where necessary. It is thus possible to assess each pupil's progress from various viewpoints. A quick totaling of diligence grades gives an overall assessment of the effort made. Comparisons can be made between subjects and from time to time within the same subject. The addition of an attendance grade highlights the importance of good attendance in maintaining progress. (The suggested follow-up procedures vary from A1 'letter of commendation to parents' to C6 'Parents interview'.)

Taken together with exercise book checks and homework checks these constitute a most detailed monitoring of the curriculum and effectiveness of the teaching programme. Pupils fail for a variety of reasons and it is too easy to ascribe this to poor motivation or lack of innate ability. We forget perhaps that poor school organization or ineffective teaching can also be contributory factors. School facilities are provided for all pupils, indeed without ROSLA many schools would not have obtained the extra buildings and other resources. This places a heavy burden on the school organization to attempt to achieve success for all.

A further development has been the establishment of a Curriculum Working Party, consisting of staff from all school departments, to investigate the introduction of a language policy for the school on the lines indicated by the Bullock Report. Following a staff conference (held on an occasional day) one member of staff has been released from her teaching programme for the year in order to advise us on this very important area.

Mention has already been made of the need to get the right 'mix' for study groups, although several factors make this difficult. The curriculum Working Party proposed that all pupils joining the school in 1976 (270) from primary schools, should be interviewed with their parents in June, prior to their joining the school, in order to obtain the maximum information and at the same time reassure those who were somewhat apprehensive at the prospect of entering a large secondary school. The working party devised a draft *pro forma* which the Coordinating Committee amended and each house provided a number of staff. The interviews were held during three evenings and each parent was given an appointment (the interviews lasted twenty minutes). An additional evening and school day was set aside for parents who could not attend on the date allocated and in all, over 90 per cent of pupils attended with their parents or guardians. The interviews were mostly friendly affairs enjoyed and appreciated by pupils, parents and staff alike. Undoubtedly the same procedure will be followed in subsequent years.

All departments have produced structural schemes to implement syllabi and both the English department and the mathematics/science faculty have now produced comprehensive handbooks to assist staff in teaching their subject. Curriculum content is subject to very detailed enquiry by both the Lower School Academic Development Committee and the Research Committee. The latter has extremely broad terms of reference and will report its findings and recommendations to the Academic Board. The former was set up as a result of a gifted pupils working party and has among its terms of reference the instruction to see that each pupil is given a work programme suitable to his or her abilities, with special responsibility for the gifted and very able children.

Arrangements for the fourth- and fifth-years have been reappraised and new developments include short courses of one term duration and core subjects for various courses. Great effort is expended upon establishing and meeting pupil option preferences in a realistic way. The sixth form is monitored by a Sixth-Form Academic Committee and academic counsellors have been appointed to supplement the work of tutors.

The school is now well into the third year of the mixed-ability programme. Last year's examination results were the best on record which was encouraging but it would be unfair to assume this was due only to the new arrangements. Parent involvement has not been neglected although consulting 1,500 families is a difficult operation, to say the least. The school parent-teachers' association has held a series of meetings: topics have ranged over 'mixed-ability teaching', 'factors which determine success in a school career', 'monitoring the curriculum', all of which have been well attended. There is a parent representative on the governing body and as standing policy contact between school and parents is encouraged either formally (tutor evenings, subject evenings, year meetings, careers meetings, or personal interviews) or at PTA functions.

The school reprographics service publishes handbooks for first year, fourth-year and sixth-year pupils as well as regular information sheets for parents (on average twelve per year).

To date, complaints have been few: 90 per cent of our pupils are first choice, our sixth form is larger than ever, staff changes are minimal! It is true to say that Hounslow Manor is not a fully mixed-ability school. The balance is about even between mixed ability and broad, or course setting. Perhaps this is because we approached the problem from a practical viewpoint rather than a doctrinaire one. I am not a social engineer by inclination, neither do I denigrate those who are. I believe that a comprehensive school should offer a range of programmes broad enough to satisfy the needs of each of its pupils and that the school should aim to provide opportunities for all pupils to achieve the highest standards, whilst at the same time encouraging to the full each one's development as an individual. I believe our 'mixed economy' is the best way to achieve this. Most important, however, if one is to be successful, all concerned (staff, pupils and parents) must know what is happening, feel involved and have opportunity to contribute, criticize and make mistakes. While all of our change decisions were largely made by ourselves, advisors and governors were kept fully informed. The main advisor concerned (for secondary) was always very helpful and is a close friend of the school. Time and resources must be made available, close monitoring of the curriculum must be undertaken and not least, one must learn to accept one's good fortune and smile gratefully when it is provided without charge.

5 Mixed-ability grouping at Bishop Douglass School

Michael Caulfield

Background information

Bishop Douglas was in September 1976 a group eleven school with seventy-two points, full-time teaching staff of seventy-three plus one 45/55 part-time equivalents. Ancillary staff amounted to two full-time school officers (the school has a split-site), one full-time secretary plus two and a half part-time equivalents, one full-time laboratory assistant plus two part-time in term-time and one full-time workshop technician. The school was six-form entry (192 intake in 1976), with slightly more boys than girls. There were 215 pupils in the sixth form. The school estimated that it had seventeen backward readers on entry and regarded fifteen to twenty children as more generally 'backward' while another ten were having remedial help. The problem of children with English as a second language was negligible. *Editors*

This chapter concerns itself with the story of mixed-ability teaching in one particular school. It attempts to explain why and how this method was introduced in the first three years' foundation course and, perhaps more significantly, why we remain convinced of its correctness fourteen years later. In that time we grew from a three-form entry secondary modern to a six-form entry mixed comprehensive (1969) by merging with an independent girls' grammar school. We are now on two sites half-a-mile apart, with 200 or more sixth formers of whom more than 15 per cent go on to degree or equivalent courses each year.

Most newly-appointed heads respond to their own experience as teachers in the initial organization of their schools and I was no exception. Parts of that initial approach remain: we are still wholly committed to school uniform albeit redesigned some years ago by a committee of teachers, parents and pupils. We demand and obtain a high standard of discipline from our pupils who are expected to see school as a place of all-round education which includes among other things a strong commitment to hard work and to stretching their individual potentials. We place a very high priority on parent consultation and involvement, corporately and individually. We expect pupils to be orderly, polite and considerate at all times and to see their school as a community to which they belong and shape by their developing and changing needs.

Perhaps more interestingly, the theme titles for the year-stages of: discovery (first year); exploration (second year); understanding (third year); preparation (fourth year); and appreciation (fifth year) introduced in 1963 still remain. They were intended to provide general theme names each with a dual purpose: to reflect the child's personal educational maturing as he or she progressed through the school, while simultaneously, offering a correlating influence between the differing disciplines of the curriculum. It is fair to admit they have had more success in the former than the latter and it remains a matter of some concern that pupils, here as elsewhere, continue to see each discipline as a separate entity. Teachers remain peculiarly defensive about what they see as the sanctity of their subjects, regarding very suspiciously any attempt to blur the boundaries between them. They are powerfully fortified by a battery of subject advisers and inspectors similarly committed.

The fact that the very first secondary modern intake was carefully streamed illustrates the kind of powerful conditioning one's own experience can have. It was not that streaming in my previous experience as a teacher had not raised doubts in my mind – far from it. In all my previous appointments the classic 'streaming syndrome' was evident with a highly motivated A stream forging ahead toward public examinations; a B stream living in hope of promotion or fear of demotion and therefore positively or negatively motivated and a C stream painfully aware of where it stood in the pecking order and often progressive only in its increasing hostility to school, to teachers and to the futility of both in their lives.

It mattered little whether it was a direct-grant grammar school or an inner city secondary modern; although the former had the cream of a wide catchment area in which it enjoyed considerable prestige and responded impressively with a battery of State Scholarships and

Oxbridge successes, it consistently failed to offer its C stream more than a handful of mediocre O levels. It is only fair to admit that none of us knew an answer to the problem we faced every time we taught the C stream (or its even more depressed lower counterpart in the bigger schools).

In 1964 we took our first step toward mixed-ability teaching although, paradoxically, it might be argued that in some respects it was a step toward even finer streaming. Our intake, now 120 boys and girls, were grouped in four forms of mixed ability for social and pastoral purposes. Each form belonged to one of four houses but the pastoral house system implied was no more than nominal until 1969. With the exceptions of religious education, art, craft and handicrafts and, of course, physical education and games, subjects were setted throughout the school. We were attempting to break out of the syndrome by the creation of what were intended to be happy, ability-mixed form groups in which the brightest and socially more endowed children would mix, share and help 'lift' their weaker and deprived contemporaries. We felt that the presence of a few subjects in which wholly mixed-ability teaching occurred would strengthen the 'lifting' influence.

The results were interesting and quickly noticeable in two directions. As one would expect, the setted subjects threw up the sort of situation which existed with general streaming. The bottom set offered much the same demoralized situation for teachers and for pupils. Our general experience was that virtually the same children found themselves in it and reacted similarly. The other sets displayed the same work and behaviour attitudes as one was used to with general streaming. We can recall how much hope we placed in the arrangement and how compellingly we argued its merits to parents; remarks such as 'setting allows *your* child to progress in each subject at the pace and level of his own ability regardless of his performance in other subjects' spring from old copies of parents' newsletters with embarrassing frequency. Even more unflattering are the memories of some past pupils who experienced this form of curriculum structure. The flaw in our claim was that the arrangements of sets initially was based on the primary school reports and an aptitude test in English and mathematics with the assumption that movement between sets would occur as frequently as possible. 'Classes in each subject are accommodated close to each other so that a pupil-move may take place at any time the teachers thought desirable.' In fact, the sets quickly hardened for all the reasons now obvious and movement in practice became a very minimal interchange after term tests. It would not be much of an exaggeration to say that it was probably easier for a child to change schools than sets!

Although the mixed-ability groups were inevitably affected by the existence of setting alongside, it was quickly clear that a new and much more purposeful mood existed within them. There were several ways in which this became evident.

The first and most evident is the one which even the strongest opponents of mixed-ability grouping can hardly deny. The 'mix' produced a happy classroom atmosphere, with all pupils feeling equal as people even though they knew quite well they were not equal in ability. Where a problem existed, it was a particular child, not a group or class. The evidence was particularly noticeable in the staff common room where the teachers working wholly with mixed-ability groups talked mostly of individual children while their colleagues with setted groups talked of classes. Those responsible for school order and discipline quickly noticed the 'lifting' effect on the whole year group. Very few schools today practise setting in the subjects to which we introduced mixed ability but it must be remembered we are here writing about 1964 and not 1977. In the year of the Newsom Report a mere handful of schools around the country were tentatively taking their earliest steps toward this method; those we were able to make contact with all shared agreement about its profound effects on school discipline. Pupils enjoyed their lessons more and participated more confidently in extra curricular activities associated with them. They were clearly more secure in a group which quickly formed a cohesive unit for social and educational purposes and which echoed the primary school organization they had just left a month or so before.

Second, there was the effect upon the teachers – again, it is necessary to remind ourselves of our total lack of experience with a form of teaching which had not at that time evolved any methodology or resources. No research of any depth and certainly no preparation of student-teachers in the training establishments existed to support and prepare our teachers for their new and complex task. Methods and resources which provided reasonably suitable aids in the streamed curriculum were almost useless in the mixed-ability structure. Teachers quickly found that they had to 'retrain' themselves.

Teachers began to talk to each other about such previously sacrosanct privacies, such as how they planned their lessons, what resources they had made or discovered for themselves, which methods had succeeded beyond their wildest dreams and which had proved unqualified disasters. We were, of course, aware of more widely-based discussion and development of parts of the curriculum and, indeed, were to adopt some of their results in the later extension and development of mixed ability (e.g. Nuffield combined science). But at that time 'inset' did not exist even as a word and debates – great or small – on the quality and content of education often washed unnoticed over the stony ground of staff common rooms. The period of 1964 to 1969 is remembered by 'old hands' on our staff as one of lively internal discussion between individuals and within and between departments. It was quite common for teachers to carry on such discussion into the late evening. Teachers were learning and supporting each other in a way we never experienced in the days of general streaming.

Thirdly, parents began to notice the effects upon their children. In those subjects which offered mixed ability the relief from the harsher and cruder competitiveness of the stream or set showed itself in the removal of tensions and unnecessary or unworthy motivations. Their children were no longer working largely to 'do better' than their contemporaries, but rather to extend themselves. The broadening of content which went hand-in-hand with the new methodology opened up new aspects of subjects and led their children to a new way of learning which seemed to capture their interests and imagination.

As one might expect, there were parents who felt certain reservations, usually those whose children were thought to be very able, or who themselves had had a very academic education and wanted the same for their sons and daughters, able or not. Such parents needed careful reassurance, a much more difficult task then when the system was in its infancy and only in part of the first year.

Before describing how the system developed further, it is worth stressing that the introduction and extensions of mixed ability in this school was never imposed by edict. It grew rather out of an increasing awareness that streaming in general was not the happiest or only way, socially or educationally, to organize any school, even where public examinations were of ultimate importance. It was fostered by our own experience and our discovery that a valid curriculum did not have to depend on a structure which left more than three-quarters of our pupils either bored, or in a state of permanent competitive tension. We would have been astonished if anyone had thought we were engaged in egalitarianism or social engineering; our conviction rested on the simple conclusion that children even of the same family are human beings of different abilities, personalities and characters. We would argue that mixed-ability teaching is a recognition of this individuality because the essence of the methodology is teaching the individual child and satisfying his educational needs.

Within a year or two we had recognized the values of this form of organization and other departments had embraced it. Indeed, by September 1966 mixed-ability grouping was a form of organization in all the foundation courses except mathematics, French and English. There are two observations worth making here. Science embraced mixed-ability teaching eagerly when the Nuffield combined science was introduced and has maintained its commitment to it ever since, although the organization of the third-year content altered some six years ago and reference will be made to this later. English will appear an odd subject to be seen to have held out against the general trend. The reason is that its then head of department felt unready to make the change for a further year and, in 1967, all subjects except mathematics, which delayed its change until 1972, changed to mixed ability.

There is a story which was commonly told in the late sixties about the head teacher of a large purpose-built streamed comprehensive school who returned one Friday in July from an ATO/DES course on mixed-ability teaching and announced over his school's loudspeaker system to teachers and pupils alike that the lower school would be 'going mixed ability as from September'. Hopefully, the story is apocryphal. What is true is that far too many schools rushed into this form of curriculum reorganization with less than ample preparation, let alone conviction. Some retreated as quickly from the inevitable chaos. It seems, retrospectively, that our gradualist approach was just right, allowing teachers time to accept its intrinsic values, prepare themselves mentally first and then professionally, search out, compare and gain from the experience of others within their school and outside, before attempting the method. It is often mistakenly assumed that mixed-ability grouping is just a timetable arrangement – once made, forever static – as indeed was streaming in the main.

The truth is the opposite (as our further experience will show) and constant reappraisals of content and method as well as of resources are all implicit in a decision to accept mixed-ability teaching in a subject. We find outselves now, in the Spring of 1977, in the following situation:

first year and second year: English, French, RE personal guidance, (Discovery and Exploration) history, geography, science, mathematics, music and drama, creative arts and crafts, PE and games.

All the above are taught in mixed-ability teaching situations. There is no setting and remedial education is carried on by what we call the 'casual extraction' method. Children in need of this help for any of the range of reasons remedial education is provided are given it to the extent they need it without losing their primary identification with their 'home 'groups. There is an agreement by all departments that this arrangement implies an acceptance of extraction from any of the subjects at the request of the remedial department.

The teaching and the form group are one and the same. Each new intake is divided by random means into six pastoral groups each associated with its vertical house. Groups are identified by their year and house, e.g. Discovery Campion. They form a strong sub-unit of their house and find their unity and security in a familial association with it. Newly-admitted pupils who have older brothers or sisters are automatically placed in the same house unless there are good reasons in a particular child's interests to do otherwise. In the third year (Understanding) there are slight differences. Until this year, all subjects were taught in mixed-ability teaching groups except mathematics which was, and remains, taught in sets. However, we are altering the arrangements for French so as to provide a series of broad bands, partly for the reasons which have been widely publicized although these have been in the minds of the teachers concerned for some time. An additional reason is the existence of courses in this subject based on the European studies concept, much less dependent upon the language and its structure and leading to popular CSE Mode III courses. All other subjects are taught in mixed-ability classes with science offering an integrated course in this year stage involving physics, chemistry and biology. The subjects offered at this level are identical with those in the first two years. Indeed, the three together form the common curriculum followed by all pupils in what we earlier called our foundation course.

Above this level the usual common core/options arrangement is offered. Even here certain subjects are taught in mixed-ability groups by choice of teachers, notably certain sciences. Most subjects use sets leading toward O level and CSE and the latter is offered virtually entirely on Mode III syllabuses.

While we remain wholly committed to the mixed-ability method of teaching and would think it inconceivable to use any other it is only proper in a descriptive chapter to examine the problems.

It has earlier been suggested that pupils do not find difficulties with it. Rather, it would seem to us that they take it for granted as a logical extension of their junior school experience. It should be equally strongly evident that we are convinced it has provided a motivation from hope and confidence in place of despair and tension. Our examination results vary from year to year as in most schools but remain consistently well above the national average. It is very rare for pupils to leave the fifth form without some examination success, even if for some it is a humble grade at CSE. A full range of advanced level courses are offered and a number of subjects such as English, history, economics, geography, biology, etc., run two or more sets. The school has a strong commitment to CEE which is seen as a much more purposeful teaching and learning situation than 'resit' O level courses and we offer up to a dozen subjects in this examination, more than half as Mode III syllabuses. The very size of our sixth-form entry must be some form of proof of the good effects of a predominantly mixed-ability curriculum down the school.

After our long experience, we would say that it is to the teachers that the mixed-ability curriculum presents problems. In a sense, they must accept that some price had to be paid by someone, and since it was the children who, in the main, paid it in the streamed structure, it seems reasonable to expect the teachers to pay it in the new situation. To say that mixed-ability teaching demands the best teachers is surely begging the question; it would hardly be argued by the apostles of streaming that their favoured structure makes a happy home for the mediocre, although it would be our experience that they feel less uncomfortable there than in our kind of curriculum.

The biggest problem for teachers is the lack of ancillary support in anything like the quantity the modern complex secondary school demands. In spite of the fact that a large comprehensive can represent more than a million in capital value and match a sizeable business or industrial organization, the level of support in the way of non-teaching staffing remains generally woefully inadequate. Many excellent teachers give hours a week in preparation of material, dealing with consumable stock such as issue of exercise books and texts, fetching and carrying pieces of equipment and even in repairing it and a thousand other tasks which could very easily be taken over by ancillaries if only we had them in our schools. In the mixed-ability organization where each class even at the same year-stage may require the most subtle of changes in methodology and therefore in teacher-preparation, hours of precious time can be spent by our teachers on two-finger typing, reproduction of materials, making and filing of workcards and worksheets, all of it well within the capacity of a reasonably competent ancillary.

Perhaps most head teachers who have faced cuts in staffing because of the harsh economic climate would feel less grieved if a little of the money saved could be channelled back to schools in the form of improved ancillary support.

Resources are of course much more abundantly available now than when we started more than a decade ago. Some are excellently suited to this method and certainly, in the sciences, the Nuffield combined science project adapted to our own peculiar needs made the difference which led that very important area to mixed ability. However, there is great need for more material designed for this kind of curriculum and able to offer choice of resources to teachers. Some of the best teachers base their own schemes of work on a selection from different published materials, wherever such choice exists. It seems to us that far too much time and money is spent assessing this kind of teaching and not enough providing support.

Within the classroom, there are two pitfalls of which the teacher must be wary. The first derives from the generally 'easier' discipline situation. It can be forgotten that the class is a mix of ability and the teaching content and method used more suited to a homogeneous class. One of the ways to avoid this is the building of a true team spirit in each department and the promotion of continuing discussion between its members. A way of assisting, as well as recognizing the need, is to allow some time within the school official day for departments to meet. We offer an earlier end to the day on Wednesdays and departments meet fortnightly, alternating with their pastoral counterparts. We also recognize that much can be gained from the interchange of teachers between classes, from team-teaching and from observation of others' methodology. We are developing toward a team teaching situation in a form of integrated studies but we are, as yet, only in the preparatory stages, mainly because we realize that if we get it right it will offer a powerful support to teaching in the mixed-ability grouping.

The second pitfall to be avoided is a total reliance upon worksheets and structured learning materials. Obviously, these are clearly valuable as teaching aids but one must be careful that they do not become teacher substitutes. Teacher-pupil relationships take on a new dimension of importance and any system of learning (however useful as an aid) which intervenes obtrusively harms that relationship. The role of head of department is singularly more important than in streaming; it demands above average qualities of leadership, dedication, sensitivity and awareness of what is happening in other teachers' rooms. Such people exist, but a head of department who feels he lacks something can, if he is sensibly aware of it, gain as much as he gives from discussions and meetings.

The school itself must be determinedly involved. Apart from helping the new teacher into the situation he has chosen but may not have experienced before, senior staff must be involved at all levels of discussions as well as amongst themselves. It seems to me that someone other than the head or senior deputy should have a specific and clear responsibility separated from any other for curriculum supervision. In our case, we call the post 'Curriculum Organizer' who is, with a Teacher-Tutor which is a separate post, a member of the senior staff.

Assessment is the subject of a separate chapter. We had great difficulty devising a scheme which would validly assess the effectiveness of our mixed-ability teaching. Our conclusion was that while we must loosely attach our method to the overall range of ability, we could only validly assess on an individual basis, where the teacher half-termly assesses the child's 'potential' and performance on a twin five-point scale. We define potential as the child's native ability affected by the use, or otherwise, made of it prior to the assessment. We lay great stress on the elasticity of a child's potential: it can increase or decrease as affected by such things as attitude, work, personality, behaviour, environmental influences, and the quality of present and previous teaching. We use the two scales as a comparison for our own purposes and in reports to, and consultations with, the child's parents. As a monitoring arrangement, we use a non-verbal reasoning test in each of the three year-stages and, purely to prevent the 'halo' effect, we publish to staff the names (without results) only of children who would appear to be underperforming or wrongly assessed by the teacher using our own system. We take care to avoid drawing unwarranted conclusions from the tests.

In a school which has grown from a tiny secondary modern to a large comprehensive with all that means in change, we remain firmly united in our belief in mixed ability as the best kind of curriculum organization in the first three years and anywhere else in the school where teachers are keen and able to use it without adversely affecting pupils. We are not at all confident that we have achieved the optimum in all subjects, or indeed are fully exploiting the opportunities for different curriculum structures. Progress can be frustrated by any of a number of causes, not least movement of staff. Since our first tentative steps in its direction, the number of schools employing mixed-ability methods has grown out of all expectation and we have found we have much to learn from colleagues and their experience in other schools.

6 Assessment in the mixed-ability group

R. N. Deale

In a sense, I suppose, this chapter ought to be redundant: there is no real difference *in principle* between assessment in mixed-ability groups and assessment in any other school situation.

However, it must be established right away that, in the mixed-ability situation, accurate assessment by the teacher is even more important than in the more conventional streamed, banded or setted school. Once children have been arranged in groups according to ability – and it does not really affect the issue how this is done – then the teacher of the A set will expect to give them A type work and, with the D group, to adopt a gentler pace. Thus, he will accommodate his teaching to his assumptions about the abilities in different groups; provided that grouping was not, initially, made on a totally irrational basis, this provides him with some sort of a structure to support and guide the teaching.

Of course, this structure may become too rigid, confining the children within it so that they are unable to move between sets, and the different levels of teaching can, in this way, reinforce and 'justify' the initial selection.

This, obviously, is one of the reasons for preferring mixed-ability groups, but, as is the nature of things, a solution to one problem brings new difficulties in its train. The absence of the support structure given by setting, means that the teacher must accept the prime responsibility for identifying the abilities of each child in the group and for providing work at the appropriate level for each. The unstreamed group must offer the flexibility for each child to progress and develop at his own pace and the teacher must monitor and foster this development if he is to meet the needs of all the children in the group.

In the mixed-ability situation, assessment procedures have to be developed which will identify, at the extremes, not only those children who may be struggling and in need of extra help, but also the abler pupils who need to be presented with new intellectual challenges. The assessment procedures must also provide teacher, pupil and parent with feedback on progress, give information to be used in evaluating the teaching programme and the effectiveness of the teaching of different classes, in compiling school records and reports and so forth. This, indeed, is what any school assessment programme must do, but, in the unstreamed school, the teacher is faced with a class group containing virtually the whole range of ability normally found in secondary schools and with the additional complication that each child may be working to an individual programme. So, although the basic principles of assessment hold good, there are significant differences in detail and in application which justify, I hope, the writing of this chapter. Readers may, however, find it helpful to supplement what is written here by referring to one of the standard works on assessment listed at the end.

Fitness-for-purpose

The general and overriding principle which governs any sort of assessment is fitness-for-purpose. This implies, of course, that the purpose of the assessment is known but, perhaps surprisingly, this is not always the case; sometimes people have vague, unstated or conflicting aims, which does not make for precision in measurement.

It is possible to identify four main types of test each of which has a different function and will be used for a different purpose. (*Test* is here defined rather loosely as a situation set up for the purpose of making an assessment; it thus includes written tests and also oral tests, practical tests, essay tests etc. *Assessment* means any 'measurement' whether by means of a test or otherwise, of some aspect of a child's ability, attainment, personality etc.)

1 *discriminating test* – that is, one which aims to distinguish different levels of attainment as clearly as possible. Most school examinations are discriminating tests, as are public examinations like GCE and CSE.
2 *mastery test* – that is, one which aims to test mastery of a given body of knowledge or a set of skills etc. The driving test is a mastery test as are some swimming tests, tests of 'standards' in

music etc. The concept of a mastery test is thus quite different from that of a discriminating test. In the discriminating test, the idea is to separate one child's level of attainment from another's; in mastery testing, on the other hand, once the predetermined standard, or criterion, has been attained, we are not concerned with distinguishing between children. Mastery tests are often described as 'criterion referenced' because they measure attainment in relation to a criterion or standard; discriminating tests are more often 'norm referenced', that is, measuring a child's achievement in relation to the rest of the class or year-group (the 'norm') or, as in the CSE grade 4, in relation to the standard to be expected of an 'average' sixteen year old in a subject.

The mastery test, then, is essentially a pass/fail type of test – either you reach the standard or you do not – while the discriminating test recognizes a continuum of ability and places children at different points along it.

3 *predictive test* – this attempts to predict later achievements; the eleven plus is the best known example and its drawbacks are equally familiar, but, briefly, if you tell children that they are not going to be successful at school (or later), then there is a very fair chance that they will not be. Related to this type of test are *aptitude tests*, sometimes used in personnel selection.

In a sense, any test can be used for the purposes of prediction. A Level results, for example, may be used by universities to attempt to forecast likely success in degree courses but the evidence is that they are not very effective at doing this,[1] which is not surprising since they were not designed to do so.

4 *diagnostic test* – this attempts to diagnose the cause of some learning difficulty. Diagnostic tests are often individual tests, need careful administration and interpretation and are more often used by the educational psychologist than by the teacher.

The purpose for which the test is to be used clearly must affect the way in which it is prepared and marked and the way in which results are presented to children, colleagues or parents. Within each of the four broad categories, we can see a range of methods from formal (examination conditions, standardized marking etc.) to informal (question and answer round the class at the beginning of a lesson, for example, to check that the previous material has been understood). This is why fitness-for-purpose is the overriding principle: some of the techniques of test construction are time-consuming and it is unrealistic to recommend that, on every occasion, a teacher should design his test with the meticulous care required, say, for the construction of a standardized reading test to be used nationally to monitor standards. At the informal end of our spectrum, we are interested in immediate feedback to teacher and pupil on the effectiveness of the teaching/learning process; in this case, it is not necessary to pay the same detailed attention to test techniques and principles as it would be when designing an end-of-term examination for the whole of a year group.

But it is important to establish clearly when the assessment needs to be carefully designed and executed, because on those occasions we must be sure that it is fit for the purpose it has to serve.

Validity

To say that a test is valid is to say that it is testing what it is intended to test. 'Describe how you would ice a rich fruit cake.' The validity of this question (set in an end-of-term examination paper in home economics for fourth-year secondary school pupils) is extremely suspect: first, you may be able to write a splendid description of the process but be extremely clumsy at doing it, and, conversely, you might be able to ice the cake beautifully but find great difficulty in describing what you did in writing. The question was intended to find out something about practical ability but has confused things by doing so by a means which involves an irrelevant factor – writing ability.

'List the woodworking glues suitable for boat-building; cabinet making; veneering.' The validity of this question is better; it aims to test knowledge of the properties of various adhesives and their suitability for different purposes. It is valid to ask pupils to show whether they possess this knowledge or not, though the question does not make it clear whether trade names or the names of types of glue are required. The validity of any question will be reduced if the children are unsure of how to answer; in this example, a pupil could get stuck because he had temporarily forgotten a brand name, when the name of the type of glue would have been enough. Or vice versa, of course, but the point is that the children should not have to guess what the tester had in mind – it should be made clear.

Another important aspect of validity is content validity, the content of the test, which should match the balance of the teaching which led up to it. If we consider the case of a public examination, we can see that it is *made* to have content validity, since teachers adapt their programmes to suit the syllabus, but, strictly speaking, this is the wrong way of going about it. Ideally, the test should follow the teaching and, in the case of most school assessments, it is not difficult to achieve this. The things to guard against are giving undue weighting to one aspect of the course – the most recent piece of work, perhaps – and not covering the whole of the course fairly. It is a useful device to draw up a test specification, or blueprint, showing the number and type of question to be set on each topic and the weighting to be given to each.

Validity is too important a matter to be treated briefly here, however, and readers are referred to the standard works on testing for further consideration of validity in test design.

Reliability

To say that a test is reliable means that it is consistent and would give the same results if the same children could take it again under the same conditions.

We can never do this, of course, (though there are ways in which we can get near) because the children are never the same. If we try to retest, some will, inevitably, have learned (or forgotten) something in the interval – indeed, merely taking the test the first time, will enable some children to learn something from it.

However, this highlights one important source of variability in testing: the child who is being tested. Naturally, children's performance varies from day to day and can be affected by all manner of extraneous factors. There is very little that can be done about this, except to take into account any known outside influences when interpreting test results, to investigate further if there are any sudden changes in a child's performance and not to place too much reliance on a single result, but to look rather for a trend over several assessments.

The second source of unreliability is in the test itself. Obviously, you can hardly test everything and any test will have to 'sample' the course that has led up to it. When you set a test, you choose perhaps twenty to thirty questions which you try to make as fair as possible. It would be easy enough, however, to set a different set of questions which would be equally fair and valid, but which would have a different effect on certain children. Thus, for one child, the particular set of questions chosen may be just the 'right' ones and he scores well, while a different set could have the opposite effect.

Unreliability from this source is accentuated by a short test which (unless the subject content to be covered is minimal) must sample very severely. Other things being equal, a long test will be more reliable – and more valid – than a short one.

The third source of unreliability is in the marking. In the case of an objective test (multiple-choice and related types), the marking would be expected to be completely reliable, that is, we would get the same result no matter who marked the paper or how often it was done. In a short answer test, where only a word or so is needed to answer, we would also expect high reliability in marking, but if we think of essay-marking, for example, it is plain that the same level of consistency cannot be expected.

In areas where subjective judgments are needed, we can never expect complete reliability, but it is all the more important to do whatever we can, to reduce unreliability to the minimum. A careful specification of the qualities to be looked for in the answers will help, as will a detailed mark scheme. Structured or multi-part questions, rather than completely open essay subjects will also make for more reliable marking and, if it is possible, multiple assessment, using the combined judgments of two or more assessors, each marking independently, will significantly increase reliability.[2] Multiple assessment is particularly desirable when testing oral work, when judgments have to be made very rapidly, or in areas where aesthetic qualities are involved, as in art.

Interaction of validity and reliability
Validity is the first consideration and must be judged in relation to the teacher's aims, objectives and teaching programme. But reliability, or rather the lack of it, must effect validity also, because with an unreliable test, the results are influenced by chance and the more chance comes into it, the less you can be sure that the test was testing what you meant it to test.

Validity without reliability is therefore not possible, but reliability on its own is pointless: it is no use being able to hit the target every time unless you first make sure that the target is the right one.

Comparability

When considering assessments in a number of different subjects, or in the same subject with a number of different classes, the question of the comparability of the assessments must be faced.

It can be argued that assessments in different subjects are *not* comparable, that a grade in, say, woodwork cannot meaningfully be compared with one in mathematics. If this is accepted, then clearly a different grade scale should be used for each subject area. This argument can become complex though, and it is harder to sustain it between mathematics and physics, for example, or chemistry and biology.

It is much more common for schools to imply – by adopting a common grading scheme for at least the main academic subjects – that assessments are meant to be comparable between subjects. And in the case of assessments in the same subject, over a whole-year group, for example, but carried out by several different assessors, there can be no question about it: there must be some sort of comparability if the information obtained is to be of use.

Although most people would accept this in principle, it is, alas, very common, in practice, to find that individual teachers adapt the grade scale entirely according to personal fancies. If a school is nominally grading on a five-point scale, A to E perhaps, it is frequently the case that one teacher does not use the highest grade ('I never give A') – apparently with some idea that this means higher standards than the rest – another will not give the lowest grade on the grounds that it is too demoralizing (though the benefit, if any, will only be apparent if other teachers do not follow suit!) and others may add pluses and minuses *ad lib*. Thus, a nominally five-point scale may be, in practice, converted into two different versions of a four-point one (B–E and A–D) or one of fifteen or more points (A+, A, A –, B++, B –, etc.)

This makes nonsense of the idea of comparability of assessments and while, within the school, we may be able to make mental adjustments, knowing that Miss X's B++ is roughly the same as Mr Y's A, pity the poor parent who has to interpret this confused and contradictory situation in relation to his child's attainments without the benefit of inside knowledge.

Mixed-ability groups

I have covered, very briefly, some of the main principles of assessment so that we can now consider how they can be applied to the mixed-ability situation. Perhaps the first issue to be considered is how the mixed-ability groups are arranged in the first place.

It is obviously undesirable to have a situation where one class in a year-group has a great imbalance of ability compared with the rest. Sometimes people go to great lengths to avoid this, using a battery of tests to try to match the proportions of geese and swans in each form. There is probably no great harm in this (provided that the children do not suffer from being overtested) but it may be questioned whether a very elaborate procedure is necessary. Even if each class is, initially, closely matched for ability, it is virtually certain that, after a year or so, this will no longer be the case. Children develop at different rates and have particular aptitudes for certain subjects; it is almost inevitable, therefore, that, after a while, differences between groups will begin to be apparent.

There is not much point in trying to achieve a delicately precise balance between groups if this is not likely to last more than a short time. The only point in doing so would be if one wanted to be able to compare directly a child's rank in one form with another in a different group. In view of the likely changes that will occur over time, and with different teaching, this would be a very dangerous assumption to make; it is much more sensible to assume that some form of standardization will *always* be needed before assessments can be compared and to build this in to the assessment programme.

Having said this, however, it would still be undesirable if all the bright children or all the slower ones were gathered in one class. Sometimes allocation to groups is made on the basis of scores on verbal reasoning tests,[3] which may conveniently be taken in the last term at primary school; this is probably as good a method as any. Primary school records would probably be equally satisfactory, dividing the intake from each feeder school randomly between the various classes and, of course, the normal adjustments (allowing close friends to remain together, separating known trouble makers etc.) would also be made.

The bases of assessment

Some people argue that any form of 'competitive' testing (i.e. any tests that produce rank orders) is antipathetic to the philosophy of mixed-ability teaching. It is important, therefore, to look briefly at the possible bases of any assessment.

Those who are opposed to rank orders may argue that assessments ought to be made in relation to each child's potential, rather than in competition with his peers. This is an attractive notion, but, in practice, we have *no* useful way of assessing potential (or even defining it) with regard to an individual child. It is not enough to rely on 'hunch' or intuition or some vague feeling that Johnny 'could do better'.

Sometimes, it is recommended that attainment should be plotted in relation to IQ scores, so that it can be seen whether a child is over- or under-achieving in relation to his 'intelligence'. However, a complex and more or less continuous debate has gone on for many years now on the validity of IQ tests and it must be seriously doubted whether they have any more than general relevance – that is to say, the scores are not of great value in assessing attainment in particular subjects.

A variation on the theme of assessment in relation to potential is to assess each child in relation to his own best work. This is perhaps a more practical basis, provided that a reasonable definition of 'best work' can be established; there will, of course, be problems when the children start a new topic or a new subject.

There is, however, a more serious objection to both these methods. If a child consistently maintains his own standard, or is thought to fulfil his potential, then he will consistently receive high grades. But this does not relate his standard of work to any other, and in absolute terms, his achievement may be very modest indeed. Parents and pupils may justifiably claim to have received misleading information if, after straight As throughout the school, they are told that this does not mean that the child can aim for a sixth-form course and the university.

If it is accepted that standards of attainment must be related, at some stage, to standards other than those of the individual child, then consideration must be given to the practical advantages of assessments based on rank ordering. At the upper end of the secondary school, standards can, in certain areas, be related to those of public examinations which give a reasonably well-understood criterion. Lower down, however, opinions and perceptions can vary; extraneous factors, such as clashes of personality, may influence judgments and it is difficult to be sure that different teachers are assessing on similar bases. In contrast to the sort of variations that may be expected in subjective judgments, the statement that a child is, say, above the seventy-fifth percentile in the year group in mathematics and science but below average in languages, gives some useful information about his abilities.

If this is regarded as 'competitive', then I would say that it is something I would be prepared to live with. The dangers of inducing an over-competitive atmosphere in a school by over-examining are, of course, real enough, but the fault lies in the school, not in the method of assessment, if it places too much stress on tests, marks, grades and minimal changes in place in the form. There can be a 'competitive' element in any form of assessment: if grade A is 'better' (in whatever sense) than grade B, then the child with A will be able to say he has beaten the child with B. It is up to the school to make sure that assessments are carried out wisely and in moderation, without arousing the feverish excitement of the final stages of the League championship.

Work units

Some courses can be arranged as a linear sequence of work units of increasing difficulty, with supplementary units for remedial purposes or for revision. In a sense, such a course would be self-assessing, that is, if the normal rate of progress was x units per term, then completion of x + y units would show above average progress and x − y (with z remedial units) would indicate slower than average.

'Completion' implies, of course, satisfactory completion, i.e. that the teacher checks to see that the work has been properly done. This would be an informal form of mastery testing and the units would need to be structured so that it would be usual for the majority of children to succeed.

Such a system should be satisfying for the children, in that completion of each unit is an immediate goal, while completion of a number represents recognizable progress; attainment is also measured by the units completed not by errors, thus rewarding success rather than penalizing failure. It provides rapid feedback to teacher and pupil and can also yield comparative information on the progress of different classes, which may be needed if setting, for example, is introduced in the upper school.

It must be said, however, that there is a risk that the most able children, given their heads, may race ahead so far that they lose contact with the rest. It may be considered desirable to bring the class together to a common starting point from time to time and to provide opportunities for the quicker pupils to work in more depth at common topics, in order to maintain the class as a coherent unit.

Test staircase

It may be felt that 'satisfactory completion' of work units is too vague a concept and that the system outlined above needs to be supplemented by a more formal test programme. Indeed, in virtually any 'linear' subject, whether the course was organized in work units or not, it would be possible to arrange a series of mastery tests, increasing in difficulty, so as to form a 'staircase', up which the children would progress one step at a time. This implies that the children would take the tests when ready for them (not necessarily all taking the same test simultaneously) which has obvious advantages. There could be problems of security, though these need not be exaggerated; with a number of tests, children taking them at different times and without a great build-up of tension (as may happen with the set-piece end-of-term examination), security should not be a major concern.

The difficulty of arranging such a system should not be underestimated. It is unusual for school courses to be structured so that criteria for mastery testing are readily apparent. This is not to say, however, that the courses might not be better if they were so structured and even the attempt to organize them in this way could well help to clarify teaching objectives – for both teacher and pupil.

Course-work assessment

Some people would prefer to rely on continuous assessment of work done during the course, rather than a programme of tests. This type of assessment should be more valid (covering all the work done) and more reliable (assessment spread out over a period) than a single test or examination. The question of comparability of assessments, however, becomes particularly important in this area.

Within a subject, different teachers of the various classes in one year may be assessing on different bases: to give a simple example, if, in one class, there are no As, is this because that teacher is temperamentally averse to giving an A, is it because that group has, by ill luck, no very able children in it, or is it because they have had poor quality teaching? If the latter is a possibility (and there can be few schools where all the teachers are equally capable), then is it possible that the situation could also exist where As *are* given, but where the children's attainments do not match those with a similar grade in another group? The school's assessment procedures ought surely to provide some sort of answer to these questions and possibly also a remedy.

Continuous assessment needs to be planned just as carefully as any other kind but some of the problems associated with it are peculiarly intractable. It is worth considering the use of a moderating test in conjunction with course-work assessment, because this can give something of the best of both worlds.

Use of a moderating test
A single test can be used as a moderating instrument to scale assessments made by different teachers so that they can be compared or combined. The justification is that we wish to retain the advantages of course-work assessment, with its better validity and reliability and because we can avoid the upset and the tension of a set-piece examination; the class teacher is, after all, best placed to know the strengths and weaknesses of his pupils, under the normal conditions of the classroom and over a considerable period. He is not particularly well-placed, however, to relate their standards to those of other classes and so we can use a single test, taken by all groups, as a sort of yardstick by which to scale each teacher's assessments appropriately.

Clearly, if we are to achieve comparability between assessments, *something* has to be common. Either:

(a) we assume that the spread of ability in each group is the same so that fifteenth place in group A is the same as fifteenth in group B, or that there will be the same proportion of grade

As, Bs, Cs etc. in each of the groups. As already noted, this is a very dubious sort of assumption to be using.

or (b) we assume that all teachers are assessing to a common standard. This can be achieved (though not easily) by trial markings, discussion of criteria, exchanging sets of work etc.

or (c) we use a common test to scale assessments.

Indeed, although I have set these out as alternatives, they are not really so. Ideally, all three approaches ought to be used: thus, we would try to ensure, as far as possible, that groups are roughly matched in ability, we should take steps to ensure that all teachers are assessing on a similar basis, and we can also use the moderating test as a back up in case something has gone wrong.

The use of a moderating test is common in public examinations both in this country and abroad, though it is perhaps not very well known as a technique within the school. The mechanics of using it are not difficult to grasp, though to explain it would take more space than is available here; readers are referred to the bibliography for details.[4]

It must be stressed, however, that using a test in this way means that we must be able to rely on its validity and reliability. Content-validity is likely to be particularly tricky because of the different amounts of work covered by pupils working, wholly or partly, to individual programmes.

Nevertheless, the problems are not insuperable: although individual programmes may be followed, it would be hoped that they are not completely random and that there is some common theme running through the year or term's work. In this case, the common test would concentrate on this core of knowledge, skills or concepts to which all pupils would be expected to have had some exposure, though the depth of study and detail would vary.

If this is not the case, then the course must be so unstructured as to cast serious doubts on its value and there is no way in which assessment techniques can be expected to remedy defects in course planning or teaching – though they can certainly make it apparent if such defects are present!

It is normal to look for a degree of correlation between two assessments before using one to moderate the other. Correlation is a statistical measure of the similarity of two orders and is expressed as a decimal ranging from + 1·00 (complete identity) through 0·00 (no relationship) to − 1·00 (complete opposites). It is usually accepted that a correlation of about 0·6 or 0·7 indicates a degree of similarity which justifies the use of one assessment to moderate another.[5]

It is almost impossible in educational measurement to get a perfect positive correlation (+1·00) but figures in the 0·6–0·7 region show that, in general terms, the two measures are in the same sort of area. There can be considerable variation, however, in the grading of individual children within this sort of correlation which is why we may want to retain both course-work assessment and the test. (The results of the moderating test may be combined with the course-work assessments, which makes use of both types of information, or they can be used just for scaling purposes and then discarded; it is simply a matter of choice.) And even with a high positive correlation, the *standard* of marking may be different: marks of 10, 9, 8, 7 and 6, 5, 4, 3 would have a correlation of +1·00.

The use of a moderating test together with course-work assessment can, then, achieve a number of desirable ends: we can retain the flexibility and other advantages of continuous assessment and overcome the problems of comparability as well as the unreliability associated with a single point of testing.

Children with reading difficulties
Conventional educational testing relies almost exclusively on written techniques and it has been tacitly assumed above that this will be the method used. In the case of the 'main stream' academic subjects, the assumption is not wholly invalid, since access to knowledge is, in the present state of organization of our society, still very largely through the medium of print.

Nevertheless, there will be some children for whom reading difficulties invalidate the conventional test paper. Oral testing is an obvious answer, though it is extremely time-consuming; in course-work assessment, of course, the teacher has the flexibility to adopt a mixture of methods as appropriate to each child. Another not wholly satisfactory compromise (for short-answer or multiple-choice tests) is to put the test on an OHP transparency and for the teacher to read out each question as it comes up. An alternative, if listening booths are available, is to provide a tape-recording of the text for slow readers, or for the teacher to read through the paper with the slower group, though care must be taken that such devices do not offer significantly different conditions of testing for some children (e.g. in the time available).

I am quite ready to admit that these are expedients and that there are, as far as I am aware, no really satisfactory answers to the problems. What it comes down to is that some children may be outside the range of our testing methods, though it is to be hoped that the number to whom this will apply across all subjects will be small.

Grades

I have already referred to the difficulty of ensuring that all teachers in a school use the same grading system. It is important, if parents and pupils are to be given meaningful information, that a common scale is used – where the assessments are made on a similar basis – or different scales if the assessments are not meant to be comparable.

It is common to use a five-point scale, A–E, which probably gives enough information if it is properly used. If my earlier arguments in favour of rank ordering within a year group are accepted, then it is reasonable to adopt some system such as A for the top 10 per cent, B for the next 20 per cent, C for the middle 40 per cent, D for the next 20 per cent and E for the last 10 per cent. This will approximate to what the statisticians call a 'normal distribution'. There is, however, no particular virtue in keeping to this pattern and a straight division of 20 per cent in each grade would be equally satisfactory. It is much more important to make sure that whatever scheme is used, it is used uniformly and without personal modifications by individuals. (Allowance should always be made for variation from any norms of this sort. It should not be done on hunch alone, however, and if a teacher feels that a group is markedly above or below average, he should have evidence to back his assertion.)

This point must be stressed as particularly important in the mixed-ability situation. In the streamed school, parents will, quite reasonably, assume that a child in the A stream, provided there are no really damning comments for teachers, is doing fairly well, even if the gradings are not comparable. The parent of a child in the unstreamed school has no such understanding to fall back on and the school must make sure that its information system provides what is needed.

Assessment of attitudes

A test can measure only part of a child's ability; similarly, assessment only of attainment in a subject may be felt to be insufficient and it may be thought desirable to include other aspects such as effort, interest, enthusiasm etc. as well. This question is debatable: some people would argue that effort, if well directed, must be reflected in high attainment and that it is not possible or necessary to assess it separately. Others would say that it is a worthwhile teaching aim to arouse interest and that therefore the degree of enthusiasm shown by the children should be assessed.

It is not intended to go into this debate here, but simply to urge that, if an assessment is to be made of any aspects of a child's education, then it should be based on observable manifestations of the child's behaviour. 'Effort' is not really observable in a global sense, so it would be necessary to specify ways in which effort might be shown: the amount of research done for a project, regularity of homework, extra work undertaken out of school etc. It would be difficult to make a complete specification and it might be necessary to supplement the evidence by subjective judgment, but it seems likely that this judgment, being based at least partially on evidence, will be sounder than one which is based only on personal feelings. It is likely too that the children, if they know what is being looked for, will respond by directing their energies in profitable directions.

It is clear, however, that assessment of attitudes should be made on a different basis from assessment of attainment. A quick look at a few school reports will suggest that this is not always the case. Where there is an 'effort' grade and an 'attainment' grade, assessors seem to follow one, or a combination of two methods: in one, the two columns are almost identical and in the second, the 'effort' grade is used to reward those whose attainment is not very high. There is a third camp, perhaps, of those who always give A for effort, saying, in effect, 'If they didn't work hard in *my* class, I'd pretty soon sort them out!'

Consistent with what I have been saying earlier, I would maintain that this sort of confusion is aggravated by using similar grade scales for what should be very different types of assessment. It would seem more sensible to use A–E for attainment and perhaps a plus or a minus, in a separate column, to show effort, or the lack of it, in reaching that grade.

There are some who would go further than just assessing effort and urge that teachers should be concerned with assessment of a child's personality as well. It must be said at once that assessment of any aspect of personality is extremely difficult. Children's attitudes can change rapidly, often in response to the personalities of different teachers or to influences outside the school. In certain sensitive areas, children may provide misleading information, either attempting to give the 'expected' answer or because they are unwilling to reveal their true feelings. And again, children may believe that they have a certain attitude towards a problem which exists for them only in theoretical terms but find out their true feelings when faced with the reality of the situation.

Attempts to probe deeply into the personality may be dangerous and damaging to the child and it has been shown that, even when conducted by trained psychologists, the results of such investigations can be unreliable and often misleading.[6] It may be concluded, therefore, that the assessment of personality within a school should be confined to areas such as effort, interest etc. which have a direct bearing on educational attainment and which may properly be the subject of comment in an end-of-term report. Finally, on this topic, it should perhaps be added that comprehensive reports on personality often reveal more about the personality of the assessor than the assessed.

Conclusion

In reviewing what I have written on assessment in mixed-ability groups, I am very much aware that I have provided no easy answers, no ready-made solutions. I make no apology for this; assessment is not a subject to be treated in isolation – it can only be considered in relation to the teaching. What I hope to have done is to outline the important principles and suggest some possible lines of investigation, but the actual work of designing the assessment programme can only be done by the individual teacher in conjunction with his teaching syllabus. It will not be easy to do, just as mixed-ability teaching is not for those who want an easy life, but I think it is worth a try.

Notes

1 See, for example, B. Choppin and L. Orr (1976) *Aptitude Testing at Eighteen Plus* NFER. 'A level is a rather poor predictor of university performance. Correlations . . . lie mostly between 0·1 and 0·4 and typically around 0·2.' (p. 13). The authors go on to point out that other predictors (e.g. O level, school reports) are even worse.

2 There have been numerous studies of the effect on reliability of multiple marking. Two useful accounts can be found in J. N. Britton, N. C. Martin and H. Rosen (1966), *Multiple Marking of English Compositions: An Account of an Experiment* (Schools Council Examinations Bulletin 12, HMSO) and in Examinations Bulletin 16, *The Certificate of Secondary Education: Trial Examinations: Written English* (HMSO 1967).

3 Information and advice on appropriate tests can be obtained from the Principal Research Officer, Guidance and Assessment Service, the National Foundation for Educational Research in England and Wales, The Mere, Upton Park, Slough, Berkshire.

4 Two straightforward methods are given in chapter VI of Examinations Bulletin 32 (see bibliography), by the present author.

5 Correlation is more fully explained in almost any standard work on educational measurement, see, for example, Vernon, below. Working out a correlation can be a tedious calculation but see chapter V of Examinations Bulletin 32 for a simple method of getting a close approximation which has many advantages for use in schools.

6 Another work by Vernon (1969), *Personality Assessment: a Critical Survey* Methuen, Social Science Paperbacks, is worth reading on this topic.

References

The following books give a general introduction and are arranged roughly in ascending order of complexity:

DEALE, R. N. (1975) *Assessment and Testing in the Secondary School* Schools Council Examinations Bulletin 32, Evans/Methuen Educational

SCHOFIELD, H. (1972) *Assessment and Testing: an Introduction* Unwin Educational. (This is particularly good on standardized tests, prognostic and diagnostic tests, etc.)

MACINTOSH, H. G. (ed) (1974) *Techniques and Problems of Assessment* Edward Arnold. (Mainly in relation to public examinations.)

LEWIS, D. G. (1974) *Assessment in Education* University of London Press

THORNDIKE, R. L. and HAGEN, E. (1969) *Measurement and Evaluation in Psychology and Education* John Wiley. (An encyclopedic reference work, though referring to practice in the United States.)

VERNON, P. E. (1972) *The Measurement of Abilities* University of London Press. (This has been a standard work for many years since first published.)

7 Special pupils in mixed-ability groups

D. C. Jones-Davies

If only because their experience of it is more recent, pupils in secondary schools may claim to know more about mixed-ability groups than their teachers. The mixed-ability experience is one which every child attending a secondary school will have undergone in the primary school and, in most cases, the memory of working alongside more-able or less-able colleagues will be fresh in their minds. However, for the traditionally trained secondary teacher, the concept of mixed-ability teaching is a comparatively unfamiliar one, where the security of an approach on one front, as in the teaching of a homogeneous set, is replaced by the distinctly schizophrenic, and therefore insecure, feeling of contesting many front lines as in a mixed-ability group situation.

Age accentuates the differences between pupils and, in particular, the age/attainment gaps widen as the pupils grow older so that, although it is true to say that even in the infants school there are distinct differences between children, the possibility of a homogeneous group in the secondary school is much less likely. Secondary school teachers have a much wider range of strengths and weaknesses to contend with in their pupils and since interests and attitudes have become established and are more diverse, and motivations developed to more varying degrees, the definition of relatively similar groups, as is possible in primary schools, is precluded. The compartmentalization of knowledge and the development of learning skills, and even of subject-specific concepts, make mixed-ability teaching more difficult at this stage of education than at the primary stage. The greater diversity of activities and, consequently, the wider range of concepts and abilities needed to cope with them makes it increasingly difficult for the intellectually or emotionally impaired pupil to deal with the learning experiences afforded him. The mobility of a secondary timetable and its insistence that all pupils relate to a number of subject teachers, adds also to the impaired child's capacity to deal with a mixed-ability teaching situation and, consequently, makes the class teacher's problem greater. The classroom-based teaching of the primary school affords a degree of familiarity and therefore of confidence to both parties in the learning situation which is not possible in the migratory routine of a secondary school. This reflects also on the class teacher's capacity for dealing with behaviour problems as on his capacity for dealing with learning difficulties. Finally, literacy is the first requirement of a child entering the mixed-ability situation since virtually illiterate children can and do absorb a greater disproportionate amount of the teacher's time and attention here, than in situations where the illiterate pupil is grouped with similarly disadvantaged children and they are all taught separately. Illiteracy is a bar to a pupil's comprehension of the majority of the wide range of subjects presented to him in the secondary school.

A mixed-ability group may be theoretically regarded as a continuum of skills and attainments which could be represented graphically as a normal curve of distribution. However, due to a number of factors beyond the scope of this chapter, the mixed-ability groups encountered in secondary schools are less comprehensive of the full range of skills and attainments. Indeed one teacher's mixed-ability group may be another's slow learning group or A stream. Nevertheless, the variety of learning skills and levels of attainment represented are sufficiently diverse to cause concern to the secondary teacher and even within that band of the continuum which represents the less-able and the lowest achievers, there is sufficient variety of difficulties to invalidate any teaching programme which offers a blanket teaching or a remedial approach.

In a mixed-ability teaching group it is possible to identify a number of different remedial and behaviour problems. It is imperative that this fact is recognized and remedial measures established to cater for the individual needs of the different types of problems encountered.

The diversity of problems is the result of the fact that a pupil's inability to make progress at school may be the result of one or more of a number of different factors affecting him. A pupil's progress may be dependent on general ability, perceptual ability, emotional adjustment, social and cultural influences, and physical health – all factors which are capable of a multitude of manifestations and, consequently, a wide variety of resulting learning and behaviour patterns. It is, however, possible to identify some types of remedial and behaviour difficulties to be encountered in a mixed-ability group and, since provision within such a group will depend on the identification of the differing needs of pupils within the group, it is necessary here to record the problem types which may be encountered and their respective requirements.

Learning and behaviour problems
ESN(M) and borderline ESN(M) pupils
Despite the development of special education in terms of special schools for ESN(M) pupils, a number of such pupils are still present at most comprehensive schools. This may be due to the fact that an individual authority's provision for such pupils is not adequate, that the authority's referral and assessing procedures and services are below strength, because some primary schools have retained their learning difficulties rather than refer them for the proper special educational treatment, or because parents have objected to special education and the removal of their child from the ordinary school. The ESN(M) pupil is even less likely to cope with education in a secondary school than in a primary school since the attainment gap between himself and his peers has widened to such an extent that he is unlikely to partake at a satisfactory level of any of the secondary school's curriculum. Furthermore, the child's long history of failure will have affected his self-image and will have seriously impaired his confidence.

The ESN and borderline ESN child, despite an occasional peak of performance in some specific activity, will operate at an overall low level of intelligence. Even where such 'high spots' occur these are not, generally, likely to exceed the norm for that specific activity for his age. The pupil's thinking is primarily still at the level of concrete operations, even though the child is of secondary school age and some pupils may not be beyond the stage of intuitive thought, in their intellectual development (Piaget 1958). The child may still have his thinking dictated to some extent by his perceptions and be largely irrational in his thinking and will not have developed the ability, essential for more logical systematic thinking, to shift the emphasis from one feature of the problem to another. His own personal feelings, his moods and his attitudes will play an essential part in his behaviour and tend to interfere considerably with his learning. Where the pupil is at the stage of concrete operations, his thinking is observed to be more rational. Although his logic is still dependent on the perceivable world of things and happenings, he now demonstrates a concrete logic and will be capable of making classifications and series which allow him to progress conceptually at school.

The ESN and borderline ESN pupil will also demonstrate generally low levels of attainment in the basic subjects. His general low ability, will of course, have contributed to his low attainments but a number of other factors have also made their contribution. He will have a number of limiting characteristics in his learning repertoire such as being unable to learn through experience as well as non-handicapped children because the unfamiliar is not readily assimilated into his schemes, to use another Piagetian construct. Any child's development depends on a kind of commerce between himself and his environment which involves the assimilation of new experiences into existing schemes and the accommodation of these schemes to new experiences. The ESN child is characterized by a kind of cognitive rigidity in that he does not readily adapt in his thinking. The essential elements of experience need to be accentuated and proliferated before he is able to benefit from them.

The ESN pupil's perceptual ability is also considerably impaired, which prevents him from establishing a really effective contact with his environment, thus prohibiting his acquisition of concepts. Such a child will require a more structured experience than is readily available in the ordinary class and, in addition, attention will have to be given to his learning habits since, in the main, an ESN pupil is a poor looker and a poor listener. Obviously, failure itself will have contributed to this and his motivation will be diminished.

An ESN pupil is also socially and emotionally less mature than his peers upon his admission to a secondary school and continues to be so unless particular heed is paid to these aspects of his development. His competence in dealing with the routines of a secondary school is impaired and it is often the case that such children, rather than adjust, become more and more bewildered. His confidence in approaching adults who are largely strangers to him is at a sadly low level. The ESN and borderline ESN pupil will, in the main, regret the passing of his primary school days.

Children of below average ability

Although children in this group have, in the main, the intellectual ability to support a sufficiently efficient level of literacy and numeracy, a number, nevertheless, have such low attainments that they will present a considerable problem to the organization of a mixed-ability group. Although these children are not educationally subnormal in the strict sense of the term, they have, nevertheless, a number of learning difficulties in addition to a basic low general ability. Depending on the cause of their impaired intellectual ability, a number of such children will have quite severe perceptual difficulties and a number will have the same learning difficulties, in terms of a failure to organize learning skills, as have ESN children. They will have the same problems in establishing concepts through the process of interaction with the environment, as will ESN children and their basic concepts will, likewise, be poorly developed.

Very many of these children will have been discouraged by continual failure in the primary school and will have lost much of their motivation to learn. Because of their very basic learning difficulties, the majority of such children will have failed to respond adequately to teaching as it is organized in a conventional primary school class with numbers often in excess of thirty-five. Furthermore, the rewards of a conventional primary school class, naturally, will have gone to their more able and responsive colleagues, thus settling the child into an attitude of failure. The development of a pattern of failure will often have led to conflict between the child and the school and the school and the child. The emotional state of the pupil will often reflect his failure and the re-establishing of confidence in teaching methods and in his, albeit limited, learning skills is an essential prerequisite of progress.

In mixed-ability groups these pupils may well be more problematic than ESN pupils because their difficulties are not as clearly defined, and their deficiencies are often disguised by a facade of superficial understanding and half-gathered knowledge. Whereas class teachers are likely to come to terms quickly with an ESN pupil's learning difficulties, this group of children often arouse frustration in teachers and are labelled 'lazy'. Such pupils' learning difficulties need careful analysis with the assistance of an educational psychologist.

In order to prevent such a pupil becoming alienated from the

school system because of his learning difficulties and his development of a low self-esteem and, often, feelings of antagonism towards
school in general, regular reassurance to compensate for the experience of failure should be organized as part of his overall remedial
programme.

Specifically retarded pupils

The two groups of pupils already discussed are characterized by a
general backwardness, despite having some peaks of attainment
amongst their generally low overall achievement. The third group of
pupils which might be encountered in a mixed-ability group will
have, despite good general intelligence, a specific retardation with
respect to a particular area of academic functioning. The reason for
such a specific retardation may be either intellectual, in the main the
product of an impaired perceptual system, or emotional.

A small number of children in a mixed-ability group can be expected to have problems with reading and spelling, not because of
general low ability or because of an emotional problem, but because
their perceptual skills are impaired in such a way as to prevent them
dealing successfully with the written work. They will have difficulty
in building up and breaking down those patterns of symbols and
sounds which make up written English.

Other pupils will find difficulty with certain academic subjects
despite showing good basic skills. It is likely that some pupils will
have become emotionally alienated from a particular subject or
group of subjects. The cause of such an alienation need not necessarily be a complex one. For example, all of us have, from time to time,
taken a dislike to something because of some trivial but temporarily
quite disturbing experience associated with the object of the attitude.
Katz and Scotland (1959) describe such a response as a proximal
attitude, namely a dislike of something might be the result of its
momentary, but strong, association with some unpleasant experience.

In both these different types of specific retardation, the establishment of a good teacher-pupil relationship is essential. Often this is
sufficient to help a pupil overcome his retardation, if it is a manifestation of a proximal attitude. On the other hand, specific retardation which is the result of a severe perceptual deficit in the child,
needs special perceptual training programmes which are applied
after a full analysis of the child's learning difficulties have been

undertaken. Such a specialist programme, although it can be carried out by a sensitive teacher not trained in remedial work, requires the overall guidance of a remedial specialist.

Pupils characterized by such perceptual difficulties are often alert and responsive and may have good oral ability. However, their virtual illiteracy precludes them from benefiting from the conventional class teaching of a mixed-ability system and, consequently, remedial action in parallel with general class teaching is essential.

Pupils with a history of discontinuous education

The frequent change of home and school suffered by Services children is labelled 'turbulence' (McIntosh 1972), and is recognized for its disturbing influence on a child's attainments. Such 'turbulence' is not reserved for Service children and we might add to the estimate of 200,000 children of Service families in ordinary schools, the 40,000 children of gypsy and canal boat families, the countless children whose education is interrupted through ill-health and the even greater number of pupils who have developed patterns of truancy. The education of all these pupils suffers from what may be called 'discontinuity' which is considerably greater in its effect than is generally imagined because order and continuity is an important element in development and education and when absent will severely affect school progress.

McIntosh (1972) writes that

> Turbulence translates the pupil from a known, stable and usually secure environment to a new and different milieu where he has no recognized status. The mobile child is the newcomer who is constantly adjusting to a fresh situation; whilst individual periods of social reintegration may be long or short, they are usually painful.

The child whose education has been affected by absences or changes of school may also, therefore, be emotionally disturbed and the discontinuity in his education will have resulted in considerable gaps in his learning, not only in the acquisition of knowledge, but also in the development of important concepts. The problems of such children have to be borne in mind in the organization of any mixed-ability group since their preparedness for learning and the levels reached in attainment may be so affected as to make it difficult for them to become effective class members. Their attainment levels will need to be established and an examination will have to be made of the concept difficulties which underlie their low attainments.

Maladjusted pupils in mixed-ability groups

Although the children outlined above may have associated adjustment difficulties, such problems will have arisen as a result of some other more basic difficulty. There could well be, however, in any mixed-ability group a pupil or a number of pupils whose adjustment difficulties are so severe as to warrant the classification 'maladjusted'. Indeed, ordinary schools play a considerable role in the management and education of ascertained maladjusted children alongside special maladjusted schools. The official *Statistics of Education, Volume 1 Schools, 1974* states that 3,566 children ascertained as maladjusted were attending ordinary schools, only 1,276 of these being in special units (DES 1975). This figure approximates to the number of ascertained maladjusted pupils attending special schools. The problem of maladjustment in ordinary schools is an even greater one, if a wider definition of maladjustment is accepted. Brittain (1970) states that: 'those children are maladjusted whose behaviour is developing in ways which have a bad effect on themselves or their fellows, and cannot be remedied without specialist psychiatric or psychological help, by their parents, teachers or other adults in ordinary contact with them'. This definition will include all children attending child guidance clinics and although the vast majority of these children will not be classified as maladjusted, they will, nevertheless, have such adjustment difficulties as to make their management and education difficult within an ordinary school. It is interesting to note that only 16,130 pupils (2,133 of these in units in ordinary schools), of the total of 74,700 pupils receiving treatment under child guidance arrangements, were, in fact, attending maladjusted schools or awaiting places at such schools in 1971-1972. (*The Health of the School Child 1971-1972* DES 1974.)

The maladjusted pupils encountered in mixed-ability groups will present a variety of difficulties, all of which will militate against successful learning and teaching. Some children will be aggressive, others will be withdrawn. Some children will be defiant, others will be over-solicitous of the class teacher's favours and attentions.

Whatever the manifestation of the basic adjustment difficulty, the amount of time required for the teaching of such children, unless special arrangements can be made, will be prohibitive to their placement in mixed-ability groups. Their exclusion, however, is not always practical and special arrangements will be required for their educational and emotional needs.

Disruptive pupils in mixed-ability groups

The recent increase in disruptive behaviour in ordinary schools, and especially in secondary schools, cannot, I feel, be attributed to maladjusted pupils. A distinction needs to be drawn between 'disturbed' and 'disturbing' pupils. The former have been described above, but the latter, although demonstrating aggressive and disruptive behaviour may not be described as 'pathologically disturbed' but are rather demonstrating an anti-authority attitude.

Whereas schools have always encountered difficult behaviour, the increase at present observed, is, I feel, due to the fact that authority at national and international level has ceased to exercise that control over the behaviour of individuals and groups that it previously found possible to do. This failure is daily illustrated in the media and has caused some pupils in schools to deny the right of teachers to exercise authority over them. The questioning and challenging of a school's authority by adolescents, is, probably, a product of their development, since adolescence itself involves a rejection of the submissive role and the seeking of a separate self-identity which, in the process of development, clashes with authority. Such clashes are evident in pupils' school and home behaviour and in terms of adolescent psychology, disruption may be described as a confrontation and a power struggle between the emerging personality of the adolescent and the school and the parental wish to retain authority according to established practice. Very many schools, and parents also, guide and provide opportunities for adolescents to achieve a satisfying and functionally successful sense of self. Inevitably, however, since adolescence is essentially a state of disequilibrium, communication between the young person and the school and/or the home does not always allow for a considered and understanding shift of opinion by the latter. All too frequently, schools and parents find themselves in a situation in which they have to assert their authority, although they are aware that in so doing they may be exacerbating the crisis that exists between them and the adolescent. Adolescence is an aggressive period, which is not to say that its nature is either violent or destructive. The aggression of adolescence is primarily assertive. This assertiveness contravenes the accepted codes of behaviour in schools and precipitates crises.

Mixed-ability grouping, however, if successfully undertaken, and practised with pupils' psychological needs in mind, can reduce the number of conflict situations. By providing relevant curriculum opportunities and affording flexibility in the organization of classroom behaviour, mixed-ability grouping can more easily satisfy the adolescent's desire for more self-directed learning.

Having thus defined the broad learning and behaviour types which may be encountered in mixed-ability groups, the principle of the need for appropriate provision for pupils according to the underlying cause of their difficulties is established. The consequence of this is considerably greater than a determination to provide learning opportunities and materials according to their level of functioning. It commits the teacher to seek remedies for the difficulties presented by each child and to forego the usual didactic philosophy of the secondary schools and substitute instead a therapeutic approach. Children with learning difficulties may not be 'taught at' as may pupils whose learning abilities are unimpaired. The underlying causes of failure must first of all receive attention, so that pupils will be more ready for teaching. Bearing in mind that pupils will differ not only in the level of their attainment in mixed-ability groups but also with regard to the factors which have caused their low achievement, either generally, or in specific subjects, a need exists to devise personal programmes, which will allow for the identification of differences, the correction of impaired learning skills and, ultimately, the teaching of subjects to the optimum level allowed by the pupils' abilities and motivations. Although it is assumed that the mixed-ability exercise will attempt to integrate, for as long as possible in a school week, the full range of abilities and attainments encountered in a secondary school, it is, nevertheless, to be admitted that, in order to operate an effective remedial system, some withdrawal of pupils will, inevitably, be necessary. It should be stressed that such withdrawal should be undertaken only in the light of knowledge of pupils' attainments and learning inadequacies since block withdrawal of pupils demonstrating a wide range of attainments resulting from a variety of causes will make the amelioration of those learning problems more difficult. Where pupils are not withdrawn individually, they should be withdrawn in groups which are as homogeneous as possible, so that a concentrated remedial attack may be made on their deficiencies in skills and attainments.

Remedial action for the 'special' pupils in mixed-ability groups exists on three levels:

1 the amelioration of weaknesses in skills underlying the basic subject
2 remedial work in literacy and numeracy
3 remedial work in specific academic subjects, effectively a 'catching up' exercise.

Individual children may well have remedial needs at all of these levels at any one time. It is important, therefore, that some attempt will have been made to closely define the remedial problem and in this respect, the educational psychologist will have an important role to play. The teacher will also have an assessment role, particularly with regard to the establishment of attainment levels and the examination of basic skill deficiencies, either by published standardized tests or by close examination of a pupil's *modus operandi*.

An Extra Learning Centre

In order to deal with these different levels of remedial needs, it is advised that a school establishes what may be called an Extra Learning Centre. Such a unit will service the academic departments or faculties of the school and will exist in close cooperation with them and not as an independent department, as is often the case with remedial departments in secondary schools. The three levels of remedial action outlined above with the wide range of remedial difficulties encountered in a secondary school will dictate the length of time which pupils will spend in such an ELC. In the case of remedial action necessary to achieve amelioration of basic learning deficiencies the pupil will require a considerable amount of time to be spent in the ELC where perceptual training and concept development activities appropriate to his individual difficulties will be undertaken. Such activities will usually bear little relation to the academic subjects taught elsewhere and are, therefore, difficult to organize within conventional subject teaching.

Similarly, amelioration of basic reading and numeracy difficulties are best undertaken on a withdrawal basis in the ELC. It should be stressed that remedial work has too often suffered from being carried out in inappropriate teaching areas and, consequently, being deprived of the resource backup which is essential if remedial work is to be successful. A well equipped ELC will include the full range of audio visual 'hardware' as well as the appropriate paper and pencil 'software'. From time to time, with the use of such equipment from the resource area of the ELC, remedial work may be undertaken within the teaching group attended by the child. This is particularly possible in English and mathematics mixed-ability groups, but the work undertaken should be in full consultation with the specialist teachers of the ELC.

The third level of remedial requirements is more likely to be met within the ordinary class subject but, from time to time, pupils may attend the ELC for remedial work when detailed individual supervision is required, or when small group work of a practical nature is necessary.

Although the ELC will have its own specialist staffing in the form of, wherever possible, qualified remedial teachers, nevertheless, the departments or faculties which it supports should be required to supplement its staffing with timetabled periods from their own timetable allocation. The responsibility for the teaching of particular subjects at whatever level rests with the individual departments and the ELC is seen to be not a separate department but a department which has an important part to play in the teaching of any subject by any other department in the school. This work will be in addition to its more conventional role of providing remedial assistance for pupils who have pronounced literacy and numeracy problems.

Furthermore, by involving all departments or faculties in its work, the ELC will encourage a comprehensive view to be taken of any pupil's problems. The coordination of academic and pastoral work will be facilitated by this method of operation and any pupil's transfer in and out of the ELC will be a matter of inter-departmental conference in order to ensure that the appropriate remedial action is forthcoming and in order that, when a child is to be reintegrated into a mixed-ability group, the teaching staff concerned are ready to receive him and are fully appraised of his work in the ELC as well as of his remaining difficulties.

The work of the ELC will also be greatly facilitated by the enrolment of non-teacher staffing in the form of volunteer adults and, when available, senior pupils of the school. The work of such 'auxiliaries' will be to ensure that individual remedial programmes, at whatever level, are completed by pupils. Such assistance will, of course, be under the close supervision of the ELC staff but the spin-off in terms of gains in basic skills as well as in general confidence and attitude has already been demonstrated (Lawrence 1974).

For pupils who have adjustment difficulties as well as for those who have become alienated from the school system and are reacting to its authority, the ELC is capable of providing the correct therapeutic experiences as well as allowing for the minimising of the confrontation situations which often give rise to disruptive behaviour. In the case of poorly-emotionally adjusted pupils, the ELC in providing individualized teaching programmes and the opportunity of working in close contact with a 'tutor' and carefully selected 'auxiliaries', will relieve the pressure that such pupils feel in a class unit, whether mixed ability or not. For many of these pupils, and particularly for the ESN and borderline ESN amongst them, the ELC experience will be for a part of the school week at least, reminiscent of support that they found available in their primary schools and which could only be reproduced in a secondary school by the formation of a special class which is precluded by the concept of mixed ability. For 'disruptive' pupils, i.e. those who are alienated to the authority of the school and who are not necessarily pathologically disturbed, the ELC will provide the opportunity of a more relevant curriculum based on individual requirements which can go some way at least to satisfying such pupils' adolescent impulses for personal aggrandizement. Even pupils who do not specifically require remedial assistance but who are disruptive of normal class routine, may be withdrawn to the ELC for supervised individual work more suited to their attitudes, or may be programmed to work outside the school either on a community project or on some work experience exercise under the direction of the staff of the ELC.

The ELC will require in terms of accommodation, according to the size of the school and the demands to be made upon it, a suite of rooms which will allow for a multiplicity of teaching exercises, including facilities for some practical work. The principle that remedial work can only be effectively undertaken in a planned environment is now receiving increasing recognition and since the ELC is considered central to the operation of all other departments or faculties within the school, the expenditure of capital on its building and equipment will more than compensate for any diminution necessary in the accommodation of other departments. Indeed, the ELC is to be regarded as an extension of every other department or faculty within the school. Its location, therefore, where this is possible in the planning of a new school, should be such as to facilitate the interchange of pupils between it and the rest of the school. This is particularly important since traffic will be continually two-way, for resources as well as clients and teaching personnel.

Conclusions

The most important principle in the provision to be made by a school organized on a mixed-ability basis for its 'special' pupils is that of individualized teaching programmes based on a detailed examination of pupils' emotional and learning impairments. The approach is more akin to that of a special school than to that of a traditional secondary school; its emphasis is more therapeutic than didactic. The most effective method providing for such pupils in mixed-ability contexts is to develop, almost on a field hospital basis, an Extra Learning Centre which can provide support for pupils within mixed-ability teaching groups and for others withdrawn from such groups for a necessary period of individualized teaching. This will require a considerable shift of emphasis on the part of a school's higher management in that it will have elevated the traditionally lowly regarded remedial department to a position of eminence amongst other departments. Furthermore the establishment of an ELC as described above, implies that the responsibility for 'special' pupils is shared by the whole school and their teaching is to be contributed to by every department or faculty.

Mixed-ability teaching is the quintessence of comprehensive education and as such must cater for all needs equally.

Further reading

A fuller discussion of the learning and behaviour problems outlined above and of ways in which slow learning and disruptive pupils may be catered for in secondary schools may be found in:

JONES-DAVIES, C. (ed) (1975) *The Slow Learner in the Secondary School: Principles and Practices for Organization* Ward Lock Educational

JONES-DAVIES, C. and CAVE, R. G. (eds) (1976) *The Disruptive Pupil in the Secondary School* Ward Lock Educational

References

BRITTAIN, M. (1970) *The Epidemiology of Maladjustment* London, Royal Society of Health

DES (1974) *The Health of the School Child, 1971 to 1972* HMSO

DES (1975) *Statistics of Education, Volume 1, Schools* HMSO

KATZ, D. and STOTLAND, E. (1959) 'A Preliminary Statement to a Theory of Attitude Structure and Change', in S. Koch, *Psychology; A Study of a Science*, 3 New York: McGraw-Hill

MCINTOSH, A. A. (1972) 'The Special Problems of Service Children' SCEA Bulletin No. 4

PIAGET, J. and INHELDER, B. (1958) *The Growth of Logical Thinking* Routledge and Kegan Paul

Select Bibliography

While each article has its own list of references, we recommend the following as a compact introduction to the present state of the field:

Surveys/Case Studies or reviews of literature with reference to ability grouping

BARKER-LUNN, J. (1970) *Streaming in the Primary School* NFER (Emphasizes the importance of teacher attitudes and the school-related benefits of mixed ability. Contains a review of the literature.)

DOUGLAS, J. E. (1972–1973) 'A study of streaming at a Grammar School' *Educational Research* 15, 140–143 (the effects of unstreaming a grammar school)

DOUGLAS, J. W. B. (1964) *The Home and the School* (streaming perpetuates the divisions of the wider society)

HEATHERS, G. (1969) Grouping *Encyclopedia of Educational Research Fourth Edition* Macmillan. Ebel, R. L. (ed) 559–570 (mainly a review of the American literature)

JACKSON, B. (1965) *Streaming. An Education System in Miniature* RKP (junior schools contrasted)

LACEY, C. (1974) 'Destreaming in a pressured academic environment' in *Contemporary Research in the Sociology of Education* Eggleston, J. (ed) 148–166 (a grammar school destreams)

MORRISON, C. M. (1976) *Ability Grouping and Mixed Ability Grouping in Secondary Schools* The Scottish Council for Research in Education (a review of the literature with particular reference to England/Scotland)

NASH, R. (1973) *Classrooms Observed* RKP (chapter 10: Scottish teachers' attitudes to pupils in a mixed-ability secondary school classroom, also interesting comments on crossed expectancies of primary and secondary teachers at transfer)

NEWBOLD, D. (1975) *Mixed Ability or Streaming? The School as a Centre of Enquiry* Pubansco Banbury School Reprographics Centre (account of Banbury Research Project)

YATES, A. (1966) *Grouping in Education* Wiley (general review of grouping including mixed-ability with abstracts of relevant research reports) including Passow A. H. The Maze of Research on Ability Grouping and Thelen, H. A. Classroom Grouping (a summary of a research project in a school where the teachers chose to teach only the pupils they wanted to)

Ongoing research
NFER Mixed Ability Teaching Project
  M. Reid, Director; L. Clunies-Ross; B. Guncher; C. Vile.
The NFER project's newsletter No. 1 contains a long bibliography including references to work in particular subject areas.
The address is: NFER Mixed Ability Teaching Project, The Mere, Upton Park, Slough, Berks SL1 2DQ

SSRC Project Teacher Strategies and Pupil Identities in Mixed Ability Classrooms: A Case Study approach B. Davies, P. Corbishley
The address is: Sociology Department, Institute of Education, 20 Bedford Way, London, WC1

Subject specialisms
The following three books represent collections of articles detailing how some subject specialists teach in mixed-ability groups
DAVIES, R. P. (1975) *Mixed Ability Groups* Temple Smith
KELLY, A. V. (1975) *Case Studies in Mixed Ability Teaching* Harper Row
WRAGG, E. C. (1976) *Teaching Mixed Ability Groups* David and Charles
A lengthy review of the latter book raising issues common to all such collections by P. J. Corbishley, and B. Davies can be found in *British Journal of Teacher Education*, Vol. 3, No. 1, January 1977

Journals
ACE *Where* Supplements
British Journal of Educational Psychology
Comprehensive Schools Committee
Comprehensive Education
Forum
Educational Research

Index

advisers, local authority 54, 68, 70
American studies 2–4, 8–10
ancillary staff 77
assessment *see* evaluation

Barker-Lunn, J. C. 8
Bennett, N. 8
Bishop Douglass School 69–79
   consolidation 74–6
   earlier history and aims 69–71
   effects of mixed-ability grouping
    72–3
   evaluation 78–9
   problems and pitfalls 76–8
   towards mixed ability 71–2
Boyle, E. 16
bright pupils 21, 45, 50, 61, 67, 81
Bullock Report 66

CEE (Certificate of Extended Education) 76
CSE Mode III 76
case studies 10–14, 55–68, 69–79
Caulfield, M. 24
class, social
   and comprehensive schools 23
   and mixed ability 32–4
   and streaming 10, 13–14
commercial subjects 22
common-core curriculum 51–2
comprehensive schools x, 4, 14,
   18–20, 22–3
continuous assessment 90–1
Corbishley, Peter 19

Countesthorpe College 19, 39n
curriculum 18–19, 20–2, 36–7, 46–7,
   51–2, 66–7, 73, 74–6, 78

Deale, Rory 45
denominational schools 22, 33
domestic subjects 22

ESN pupils 100–1, 110
English 22, 36, 60, 65, 74, 109
European studies 76–7
   evaluation *ix*, 45, 49, 53, 65–6,
    78–9, 80–97
   of attitudes 95–6
   children with reading difficulty
    93–4
   continuous assessment 90–1
   correlation 92–3, 97n
   IQ tests 88
   importance in mixed ability 80–1
   multiple assessment 85
   objective tests 85
   types and fitness 81–3, 89–92
   validity and reliability 83–6
Extra Learning Centre 108–10

gifted pupils *see* bright pupils
grammar schools 18, 33, 56, 70–1
grouping procedures 42–4, 50, 87

Hadow Report 8, 9
headmasters
   newly appointed 69
   whizz kid type 34

Hightown Grammar (Lacey) 10–14, 16*n*
Hirst, P. H. 33
homogeneous grouping *see* streaming
Hounslow Manor School 55–68
  consolidation 65–8
  evaluation 65–6
  history and organization 55–7
  timetabling 63–5
  towards mixed-ability 58–65
humanities 36–7, 63

ideology 26–7, 37
immigrants
  in America 3
  in Britain *x*, 55, 59
in-service training 48, 54, 60
individual learning programmes 45–6
intake of pupils 22–3, 56

Lacey, Colin 10–14, 16*n*
learning difficulties *see* remedial pupils
local authority advisers 54, 68, 70

McIntosh, A. A. 104
maladjusted pupils, 105–6
mathematics 20, 21, 37, 60, 63, 65, 74, 109
measurement techniques 6–7
mixed-ability grouping
  Bishop Douglass School 69–70
  bright pupils 21, 45, 50, 61, 67, 81
  curriculum 20–2, 36–7, 46–7, 51–2, 66–7, 73, 74–6, 78
  diagnostic 30
  effects 35–7, 72–3
  evaluation *ix*, 45, 49, 53, 65–6, 78–9, 80–97
  extent *v*, 20–3
  fourth and fifth year 50–2, 76
  grouping procedures 42–4, 50, 87
  Hightown Grammar 10–14

history 8–10, 18–20, 25–6
Hounslow Manor School 55–68
planning 41–54
problems and pitfalls 76–8
pupil benefits 14, 31, 37, 70, 72, 73–4, 107
remedial pupils *ix–x*, 21, 35–6, 43–4, 74, 98–112
research *vi–vii*, 3–17, 19–40
social purpose 38–9
teacher attitudes 4–5, 10, 24–6, 41, 72, 76–7
teaching techniques 45–9, 72–3
modern languages 20, 21, 36–7, 60, 65, 74
modern schools *see* secondary modern schools

Newsom Report 18, 72
non-teaching staff 77
Nuffield combined science course 74, 77

older pupils and mixed ability 50–2, 76

parent involvement 67–8, 70
pastoral care 44, 75, 109
Physical Education 42
Piaget, Jean 100, 101
planning 41–54
  curriculum 46–7, 51–2
  grouping procedures 42–4, 50, 87
  in-service training 48, 54, 60
  teaching techniques 45–9, 72–3
  timetabling 52–4, 63–5
primary schools 28–9, 72, 98, 102
pupils
  attitude to work 95–6
  balanced intake 22–3, 56
  benefits of grouping 14, 31, 37, 70, 72, 73–4, 107
  bright 21, 45, 50, 61, 67, 81
  evaluation 65–6, 78–9, 80–97
  fourth and fifth year 50–2, 76
  grouping procedures 42–4, 87

remedial *ix–x*, 21, 35–6, 43–4, 74, 98–112
  with reading difficulty, testing 93–4

ROSLA 22, 56, 66
reading difficulty, testing of children with 93–4
reading lists 17, 39–40, 97, 112, 113–4
remedial pupils *ix–x*, 21, 35–6, 43–4, 74, 98–112
  below average ability 102–3
  discontinuous education 104–5
  disruptive 106–7, 110
  ESN 100–1, 110
  Extra Learning Centre 108–10
  maladjusted 105–6
  specifically retarded 103–4
  types of remedial action 108
research 1–17, 19–40
  American 2–4, 8–10
  in context 7
  diversification 2
  international variations 2–4
  measurement techniques 6–7
  presentation 5–6
  on pupil factor 5, 10
  on social effects 3–4
  standardized testing in 2, 6, 30
  Swedish 3–4
  teacher attitudes to 1, 15
  on teacher factor 4–5, 10

Schiller, Christian 9
school uniform 69–70
schools
  Bishop Douglass School 69–79
  comprehensive *x*, 4, 14, 18–20, 22–3
  Countesthorpe College 19, 39*n*
  denominational 22, 33
  differences among *x*, 7, 12–13
  grammar 18, 33, 56, 70–1
  Hightown Grammar 10–14, 16*n*
  Hounslow Manor School 55–68
  primary 28–9, 72, 98, 102
  secondary modern 18–19, 70
  single-sex 25, 33
  Woodlands School 19, 39*n*
Schools Council
  Materials for Curriculum Planning Unit *vii*, 41
  science 22, 37, 60, 63
  Nuffield combined science course 74, 77
secondary modern schools 18–19, 70
single-sex schools 25, 33
Social Science Research Council *vi*, 19
special pupils *see* remedial pupils
standardized tests 2, 6, 8, 10, 30, 83, 88
streaming
  and class 10, 13–14
  history 8, 10
  justification 9–10
Swedish studies 3–4

Taylor, W. 19. 39*n*
teachers
  and assessment 86, 89, 91–2, 95, 108
  attitudes to comprehensive re-organization 31
  attitudes to mixed ability grouping 4–5, 10, 24–6, 41, 72, 76–7
  attitudes to research 1, 15
  in-service training 48, 54, 60
  and subject boundaries 70, 98
  turnover 32, 79
teaching techniques 45–9, 72–3
  team-teaching 78
  testing 81–6
Terman, L. M. 8
tests
  objective 85
  standardized 2, 6, 8, 10, 30, 83, 88
  types and fitness 81–3, 89–92
timetabling 52–4, 63–5
turnover, staff 32, 79

Woodlands School 19, 39*n*
workshop subjects 22, 37

Yates, A. 15
Young, D. A. and Brandis, W. 12, 13